AMERICAN

KINSHIP

DATE DUE

DAVID M. SCHNEIDER

AMERICAN

KINSHIP

A

CULTURAL

ACCOUNT

SECOND EDITION

The University of Chicago Press
Chicago and London

To ADDY

The University of Chicago Press, Chicago 60637
The University of Chicago Press, Ltd., London

© 1968, 1980 by The University of Chicago
All rights reserved. Published 1968
Second edition 1980
Printed in the United States of America

95   8 7

Library of Congress Cataloging in Publication Data

Schneider, David Murray, 1918–
    American kinship.

    1. Kinship—United States.   2.   Family—United States.
    I.   Title.
HQ535.S33   1980   301.42'1'0973   79-18185

ISBN 0-226-73930-9 (paper)

Contents

Preface

American kinship is an example of the kind of kinship system which is found in modern, western societies. This kind of system is particularly important not only because it is found in an important kind of society, but also because it is different from the kinds of kinship systems found elsewhere in the world.

The kinship systems of modern, western societies are relatively highly differentiated as compared with the kinship systems found in many primitive and peasant societies. By "differentiated" I mean simply that kinship is clearly and sharply distinguished from all other kinds of social institutions and relationships. In many primitive and peasant societies a large number of different kinds of institutions are organized and built as parts of the kinship system itself. Thus the major social units of the society may be kin groups—lineages perhaps. These same kin groups may also be the property-owning units, the political units, the religious units, and so on. Thus, whatever a man does in such a society he does as a kinsman of one kind or another. If he becomes chief he does so according to some rule of succession, perhaps inheriting the office from his father or mother's brother. If he marries a girl it is because she is a member of a kin category such as mother's brother's daughter. If he needs help with some economic enterprise, like gardening or hunting, he calls on his brother-in-law because he is the proper person to give assistance in such endeavors.

But in the United States all of these institutions are quite clearly differentiated from each other. In the United States one is supposed to earn political office by free election, not by the right of succession to the office held by one's father or uncle. One owns property in one's own right and enters into economic relations where one chooses and according to rules which are supposed to be quite free from the constraints of kinship, religion, or politics. And one goes to a church of one's own choosing, following the dictates of one's conscience and not the dictates of one's kinship group, political party, or the corporation one is employed by.

The fact that kinship is so clearly differentiated in modern, western societies has certain advantages for the study of many different problems. One of these, which has particularly interested me for some time, is the question of "the nature of kinship" in the sense of establishing just what the distinguishing features of kinship consist of. It makes particularly good sense, it seems to me, to study kinship in as close to its "pure form" as possible here in America, rather than in some other society where it is hidden beneath layers of economic, political, religious, and other elements.°

There is another reason why the study of kinship in America is especially important to Americans and that is that as Americans, this is a society and a culture which we know well. We speak the language fluently, we know the customs, and we have observed the natives in their daily lives. Indeed, we *are* the natives. Hence we are in an especially good position to keep the facts and the theory in their most productive relationship. We can monitor the interplay between fact and theory where American kinship is concerned in ways that are simply impossible in the ordinary course of anthropological work. When we read about kinship in some society foreign to our own we have only the facts which the author chooses to present to us, and we usually have no independent source of knowledge against which we can check his facts. It is thus very hard to evaluate his theory for ordering those facts.

By the same token of course we are able to achieve a degree of control over a large body of data which many anthropological field workers hardly approach, even after one or two years in the field. Hence the quality of the data we control is considerably greater, and the grounds for evaluating the fit between fact and theory is correspondingly greater.

I first undertook systematic work in American kinship in 1951, when, in collaboration with George C. Homans, I collected some genealogical materials and particularly material on kinship terminology from graduate students and faculty in the Department of Social Relations at Harvard University. Some of the results of that study were published in 1955.

In 1958-1959, when Professor Raymond Firth of the London School of Economics was a fellow at the Center for Advanced Study in the Behavioral Sciences, we proposed a comparative study of kinship in Britain and the United States to the National Science Foundation. Although the

---

° See D. M. Schneider, "The Nature of Kinship," *Man*, No. 217 (1964); and "Kinship and Biology," in A. J. Coale *et al.*, *Aspects of the Analysis of Family Structure* (Princeton: Princeton University Press, 1965).

study was to be comparative, each of us was to be free to follow lines and methods of our own choosing. We thus made no attempt to replicate each other's work precisely, although we kept in close touch throughout the course of the work.

This book is the first published report on the American project. It contains no comparative material, but deals only with American kinship. A book comparing American and British kinship is being planned now.

The funds for the field work and the analysis of the material came primarily from the National Science Foundation, whose support is gratefully acknowledged here. In addition, special aspects of the analysis, the collection of special bodies of field materials, and a portion of the write-up of some of the materials was made possible by a grant from the National Institutes of Health.

My thanks are due to Dr. Constance Cronin, Mr. McGuire Gibson, Dr. Nelson Graburn, Dr. Esther Hermite, Mrs. Elizabeth Kennedy, Mr. Charles Keil, Miss Nan Markel, Mrs. Eleanor McPherson, Mrs. Pat Van Cleve, Miss Harriet Whitehead, and Mrs. Linda Wolf, who did the field work in Chicago and who all did a very fine job of it under circumstances that were often hardly easy.

Dr. Millicent Ayoub made many important suggestions during and after the fieldwork. Thanks are due to Dr. Dell Hymes for his stimulating letters. Mr. Calvert Cottrell helped to supervise the collection of the genealogies and was primarily responsible for the quantitative analysis of that material. Dr. Gary Schwartz helped in many different ways during the collection of the field materials, primarily keeping a close watch on class and status considerations, and keeping the field workers alert to them.

I owe a special debt to Paul Friedrich, who took time from his own field work to read an early draft of some parts of this book. I learned a good deal from him about kinship and linguistics in many discussions during the course of this work. Bernard S. Cohn, Fred Eggan, Raymond Firth, Raymond Fogelson, Jane and Anthony Forge, Clifford Geertz, Eugene A. Hammel, David Olmsted, Tom Sebeok, Martin Silverman, Melford Spiro, and Raymond T. Smith all read parts or all of the manuscript at one or another stage of its writing, and I acknowledge here the many useful suggestions which they made. In addition, all the field workers whom I could contact went over the manuscript from the point of view of those who had gathered the largest share of the data on which it was based. Their help is greatly appreciated.

Finally, I am particularly grateful to Dr. Ralph Tylor, the director of the Center for Advanced Study in the Behavioral Sciences, and to Preston Cutler, Jane Kielsmier, and the rest of the staff of the Center, where the final draft of this book was written.

d.m.s.

Acknowledgments, 1980

I am grateful to Marshall Sahlins for his helpful comments on the first draft of chapter 7, "Twelve Years Later," written for this edition, and for the use of his most apt phrasing of the distinction "culture-as-constituted" and "culture-as-lived" or "culture-in-action" from his unpublished paper "Individual Experience and Cultural Order." I also appreciate the comments of Virginia Dominguez in her letter which reached me as I was preparing to write this epilogue. And I would like to thank Michael Silverstein for his helpful reading. I am also indebted to the many commentators on *American Kinship* who took the trouble to tell me not only what was wrong with the book but also what was right with it. There are just too many of them to name individually.

CHAPTER ONE

Introduction

I.

This book is concerned with American kinship as a cultural system; that is, as a system of symbols. By symbol I mean something which stands for something else, or some things else, where there is no necessary or intrinsic relationship between the symbol and that which it symbolizes.[1]

A particular culture, American culture for instance, consists of a system of units (or parts) which are defined in certain ways and which are differentiated according to certain criteria. These units define the world or the universe, the way the things in it relate to each other, and what these things should be and do.

[1] I follow Talcott Parsons, Clyde Kluckhohn, and Alfred L. Kroeber in this definition of culture and in this definition of the problem. Specifically, T. Parsons and E. Shils, *Toward a General Theory of Action* (Cambridge: Harvard University Press, 1961); A. L. Kroeber and T. Parsons, "The Concepts of Cultural and of Social System," *American Sociological Review* (1958), pp. 582-83; and A. L. Kroeber and C. Kluckhohn, "Culture: A Critical Review of the Concepts and Definitions," *Papers of the Peabody Museum* (Cambridge: Harvard University, 1952), Vol. 47, No. 1. The work of Clifford Geertz is an excellent example of this tradition, and his paper, "Religion as a Cultural System," is particularly useful for his definition of the term "symbol," which I have followed in this book. See especially pp. 5-8 of his paper, in *Conference on New Approaches in Social Anthropology, Anthropological Approaches to the Study of Religion*, ed. Michael Banton (London: Tavistock Publications, 1965). I have, however, departed from this tradition in one important respect. I have here attempted to deal with culture as a symbolic system purely in its own terms rather than by systematically relating the symbols to the social and psychological systems, and to the problems of articulating them within the framework of the problem of social action. My debt to Claude Levi-Strauss is obvious; my debt to Ruth Benedict's "Chrysanthemum and the Sword" (Boston: Houghton Mifflin Company, 1946), less obvious but quite as great. The work of Louis Dumont has been an especially valuable stimulus.

1

I have used the term "unit" as the widest, most general, all-purpose word possible in this context. A unit in a particular culture is simply anything that is culturally defined and distinguished as an entity. It may be a person, place, thing, feeling, state of affairs, sense of foreboding, fantasy, hallucination, hope, or idea. In American culture such units as uncle, town, blue (depressed), a mess, a hunch, the idea of progress, hope, and art are cultural units.

But the more usual sense in which the term "unit," or "cultural unit," can be understood is as part of some relatively distinct, self-contained system. American government is a good example. There is national as against local government and they stand in a special relationship to each other. National government consists of an executive branch, a legislative branch, and a judicial branch—again, units defined and placed in relationship to each other. One could go on along the line noting and naming and marking each distinct, cultural entity or unit—its definition, the conception of its nature and existence, its place in some more or less systematic scheme.

It is important to make a simple distinction between the culturally defined and differentiated unit as a cultural object itself, and any other object elsewhere in the real world which it may (or may not) represent, stand for, or correspond to.

A ghost and a dead man may be helpful examples. The ghost of a dead man and the dead man are two cultural constructs or cultural units. Both exist in the real world as cultural constructs, culturally defined and differentiated entities. But a good deal of empirical testing has shown that at a quite different level of reality the ghost does not exist at all, though there may or may not be a dead man at a given time and place, and under given conditions. Yet at the level of their cultural definition there is no question about their existence, nor is either one any more or less real than the other.

In one sense, of course, both ghost and dead man are ideas. They are the creations of man's imagination or intellect, which sorts certain elements out and keeps others in, formulating from these elements a construct that can be communicated from one person to another, understood by both. Yet at that level of reality the question of whether one can actually go out and capture either a ghost or a dead man is quite irrelevant.

It would be an error and oversimplification to say that the objective existence of the ghost is lacking, but the objective existence of a dead man can sometimes be established; in that way at least the dead man can exist but the ghost cannot. It would develop this error even further to say that ghosts cannot exist but dead men can. Even though such a statement is certainly true at one level of discourse, it misses the whole point and the whole significance of cultural constructs, cultural units, and culture in general.

Both "ghost" and "dead man" are words, of course, and it is certainly important to note that words "stand for" things. As mere disturbances in the atmosphere which are heard, or as mere distortions of the otherwise placid surface of a page which are seen, they nevertheless remain words which stand for something.

But the question is not *what thing* they stand for in the outside, objective, real world, although with a word such as "dog," we can take that concrete animal, stand him on the ground, point to him, and say, "That is a dog." The question is rather *what different things* does such a word stand for. The word "dog" certainly is a cultural construct—in one of its meanings—and it is defined in certain ways as a cultural unit. Its referent in that context, then, is not the "objective" animal itself, but rather the set of cultural elements or units or ideas which constitute that cultural construct.

Insofar as a word is the name for something, and insofar as the word names—among many other things—a cultural unit or construct, one might conclude that culture consists of the language; that is, the vocabulary, grammar, and syntax, or the words and their definitions and their relationships to each other.

There is no question but that language is a major part of culture. It is certainly a system of symbols and meanings and, therefore, in that sense alone it conforms to the definition of culture which I have offered. We know immediately that "ghost" is a cultural construct or unit of some kind because there is a word for it, it has a name, the word has meaning, and the friendly natives can explain that meaning and define the word.

But if language is, in one of its meanings, culture, culture is not wholly or exclusively or entirely language. Culture includes more than language because language is not the *only* possible system of symbols and meanings. This means that there can be and often are cultural units without simple, single words or names for them. It means that there are units which can be described in words and identified as cultural units, but which do not have names in the special sense of the single lexeme, as the name for the dog is "dog" or the name for the chief executive officer of the government of the United States is "President."

I am less concerned in this book with the question of whether a cultural unit has a single name or a two-word name, or can only be designated by a series of sentences, than I am with the definition and differentiation of the cultural units themselves. It is vital to know that cultural categories or units very often have single-lexeme names and that one of the most important ways of getting started on a description of those units is to get a collection of such single-lexeme names and try to find out what they mean.

It is equally vital to know that cultural categories and units often do not have single-lexeme names, and that the description of the cultural units is by no means exhausted when a complete list of names with their meanings has been assembled.

It is useful to restate this in another way. The *semantic* analysis of a system of lexemes is not isomorphic with the description of the system of cultural units or categories, even if it remains an open question whether the semantic analysis of a single lexeme within a system of lexemes is isomorphic with the analysis or description of that single cultural unit of which that lexeme may be a part.

This same point can be put very simply. The meanings of the names alone are not exactly the same as the meanings of the cultural units. This is necessarily so because some cultural units do not have names. Since this book is about the cultural units, and since the names are very important parts of the cultural units, this book uses them and deals with them; but the names are only one among many parts of the subject of the description, they are not the object of the description.

Words, as names for cultural units, are one of the best ways to begin to discover what the cultural units are. But they have one fundamental characteristic which must be taken into account. A word never has a single meaning except in one, limiting set of circumstances. When a word is being used within the very narrow confines of a rigidly controlled scientific utterance where the meaning is explicitly defined in unitary terms for that particular occasion or that particular usage, any other meanings that word might have are suppressed and the defined meaning is its only meaning. But since words are seldom used in this way, and rarely if ever in "natural" culture, this limitation can safely be ignored while the polysemic nature of words is kept firmly in mind.

Simply knowing that a word can have many meanings, and simply knowing which are the many meanings a word can have, are not enough. What is necessary to know is which of the many meanings applies when, and which of the many meanings does not apply or is not relevant under what circumstances; and finally, how the different meanings of the word relate to each other. This point, too, becomes rather important in the material which follows, so I have stated it in its most general terms here.

II.

I started with the point that a cultural unit or cultural construct must be distinguished from any other object elsewhere in the real world, and that the cultural unit or construct has a reality of its own. The ghost and the dead as cultural constructs are quite real, demonstrable elements even though, at quite another level, ghosts do not exist but dead men do. This subject soon led into the problem of the relationship between cultural units and the words which name them and to the point that a semantic account overlaps, but is not identical with, a cultural account since significant cultural categories do not always have names.

Now I must return to the starting point once more to make explicit certain other implications of the basic point that culture must be distinguished from other objects in the real world.

Certainly culture is in one sense a regularity of human behavior, and as such it is quite objective and quite real. But this does not mean that any observable, definable, demonstrable regularity of human behavior is culture. Neither does it mean that culture can be directly inferred from any regular pattern of human behavior.

Among the different forms in which symbols can be cast, one consists of the definition and differentiation of persons in interaction. This is the set of rules which specify who should do what under what circumstances. It is the question which proceeds from the fact that the members of a given culture have chiefs and counselors whom they can ask what their rights and duties are, what their roles are, what rules are supposed to guide and govern what they do. These are the standards, the guides, the norms for how action should proceed, for how people of different cultural definitions should behave.

But the cultural constructs, the cultural symbols, are *different* from any systematic, regular, verifiable pattern of actual, observed behavior. That is, the pattern of observed behavior is different from culture. This is not because culture is not behavior. Culture *is* actual, observable behavior, but of only one specially restricted kind.

An example may be helpful here. In American culture there is a culturally defined unit called "policeman." The policeman's role is defined as that of enforcing the law. One set of laws consists of traffic laws of the sort with which we are all familiar. The driver of a vehicle (another culturally defined unit) is supposed to stop at a red traffic signal, and go when the signal is green. These are all units in a cultural domain.

If the driver stops when the signal is red and goes when the signal is green, the observing policeman does not act. But if the driver goes when the signal is red and stops when the signal is green, the policeman should give the driver a ticket or a summons for breaking the law.

Now it is clear that the definition of the units and the statement of the rules is quite different from our going out on a street corner and watching the behavior of drivers and policemen. After some systematic observation we may find that most drivers, but not quite all, do not go through red lights, that they do tend to get their vehicles moving when the light turns green, and that there is some specifiable rate at which traffic summonses are issued to those drivers who do drive through red lights and who fail to move through green lights.

The distinction between the definition of the units and the rules on the one hand (culture) and the patterns of actual behavior derived from observation of traffic-light behavior on the other hand is fundamental to this book. *This book is concerned with the definitions of the units and rules, the culture of American kinship; it is not concerned with the patterns of behavior as formulated from systematic observations of each of its actual occurrences.*

What is equally important is that these two are to be understood as *independent* of each other and not as being in tautologous relationship. That is, the definition of the units and the rules is *not* based on, defined by, drawn from, constructed in accord with, or developed in terms of the observations of behavior in any direct, simple sense.

Let us go back to the traffic light and the street corner once again. How do we know that there is a rule against driving through the red light except by observing what happens? Cars generally do not go through red lights. How do we know that there is such a thing as a policeman except by observing him arrest drivers and give them summonses when they pass the red light? How do we know that the policeman is not just another driver in different clothing except by observing him giving but not receiving summonses?

When we observe a regularity in behavior, which takes place in a given situation over a period of time, and when that regularity consists of visual observations or statements by the actors themselves that there is such a regularity—"people in this town stop for red lights"—then indeed there is reason to suspect, or we may formulate the hypothesis, that there are cultural units and cultural rules entailed in that regularity.

But once again, the regularity "people actually stop for red lights" is different in a fundamental and important way from the regularity "people are by law supposed to stop for red lights." The first may or may not imply the second. And since it is the cultural units and rules that this book seeks to locate, the presence of observable regularities is only a suggestion about where to look for them. The two can and must be kept separate; the evidence for the existence of a cultural unit or a cultural role cannot rest on any observed regularity of actual instances of the behavior itself.

This is fundamentally the same problem, even in this guise, as the problem stated earlier where ghosts were the example. And the point remains that the cultural rule or the cultural unit exists at a cultural level of observation and without regard to the level of specific instances and concrete occurrences. No amount of direct observation of the behavior of ghosts themselves will yield any information about how the cultural construct of the ghost is formulated. Direct visual observation can certainly yield *hypotheses*, but only hypotheses, about the units and the rules of traffic lights as cultural constructs, but even in such a case it is a moot question whether this manner of producing hypotheses about the cultural constructs is very useful.

Since it is perfectly possible to formulate, to communicate, to describe, and to understand the cultural construct of ghosts without actually visually inspecting even a single specimen, this should be true across the board and without reference to the observability or nonobservability of the objects that may be presumed to be the referents of the cultural constructs.

But consider, now, a problem of the same order but posed in a somewhat different way. Suppose that we know that there are cultural units X, Y, and Z. And suppose that the rule is that units X and Y never appear together, but X always appears associated with Z. Now we observe what actually happens in a carefully selected sample of cases. Direct observation shows that in 32.7 per cent of the cases X and Y appear together (contrary to the rule!) and that in no instances which are observed does Z ever occur when X is present (contrary to the rule in 100 per cent of the cases!).

Do we infer that the rule is weak where 32.7 per cent of the cases deviate from it and that there is no rule where 100 per cent of the cases fail to conform to it? We do not at all. The question of whether there is a rule formulated as a cultural rule cannot be decided on the basis of such evidence. To put it simply, such evidence is quite irrelevant to the question of whether there is or is not a cultural unit, a cultural concept, a cultural rule, a cultural entity.

This problem has one other direction which should be considered. The argument might be developed in this way: Cultural units, constructs, rules, and so on are not just "given." They are not, contrary to mythology, handed down from the sky to remain in the same state until they are taken back by the gods who invented them. They arise, they grow, they change. They may or may not be responsive to the actual conditions of life, to different population pressures, to different ecological conditions, to the scarcity of food or the prevalence of disease, to the joys and the sorrows of life. One essential problem, then, is to chart the relationship between the actual states of affairs and the cultural constructs so that we can discover how the cultural constructs are generated, the laws governing their change, and in just what ways they are systematically related to the actual states of affairs of life.

There is no question but that this is one among a number of legitimate and interesting problems. But it is not the one I have chosen. I have stated the others in order to clearly distinguish my problem from other, apparently similar problems, and in order to make clear certain assumptions which are fundamental to the one I have chosen.

This problem assumes that the cultural level of observation can be distinguished from all others; that cultural units and constructs can be described independently of all other levels of observation; and that the culture so isolated can be examined to see what its core symbols are (if there are core symbols); how meaning is systematically elaborated (if it is systematically elaborated) throughout its differentiated parts; and how the parts are differentiated and articulated as cultural units (if they are so articulated).

In the most general terms, then, the problem I have posed is that of describing and treating culture as an independent system and of analyzing it in its own terms; that is, as a coherent system of symbols and meanings.

The specific objective of this book is to describe the system of symbols and meanings of American kinship. It tries to show the cultural definition of the units of American kinship as they occur in American culture. It also tries to show the rules, formulated as a part of the cultural system, that show how such units relate and do not relate to each other, the symbolic forms in which the units and their relations are cast, and the meanings attached to those symbols. It is in this sense that the subtitle of the book, "A Cultural Account," is to be understood.

III.

Given this objective, how are the cultural units located, described, and defined? By what methods are the observations made which yield cultural rules, constructs, units, symbols, and meanings? What data should be collected for this purpose and by what methods?

A psychologist may use *subjects* in his experiments, a sociologist may count his *respondents* in a survey of opinion or attitude, a psychiatrist may describe his *patients*. But an anthropologist, where culture is the object of his study, uses *informants*.

Moreover, where a sociologist may draw a *sample* of respondents, or a critic may attack the general applicability of a psychologist's results by impugning his sample, the best that can be said for an anthropologist is that he has a good *bunch* of informants. And it should be noted that a sociologist *draws* a sample or *selects* his sample, while the anthropologist is often selected by his informants. Some of the very best informants are self-selected.

These different words have different meanings and it is no accident that the anthropologist often uses informants rather than subjects, respondents, or patients, and that informants come in bunches, not samples, and that they are often self-selected.

The informant is distinguished by what it is that is sought from him and by the relationship which the anthropologist has with him. It is precisely because the anthropologist does not understand the native culture, does not know what the units of that culture are, and has only the vaguest idea as to the ways in which those units might be put together that he goes to an informant.

In a very fundamental sense the anthropologist is like a child who must be socialized. He has to be taught right from wrong according to the standards of the culture he is studying. He has to learn what to do and what not to do, how to do it and how not to do it, what is worth doing and what is not. He has to learn the names for things and what their properties are, what their values are and what dangers lurk beneath them or behind them or within them or around them. And just like a child, one of the most important things he has to learn is the language; only when he has learned to speak the language well enough does he really begin to perceive the subtleties and the full texture of the fabric of the culture he is studying.

When an anthropologist goes into the field to study a culture he generally starts by learning the language. Thus his language teachers tend to become his first and sometimes his most important informants. He works with them for long periods of time, picking up vocabulary, learning the names for things, learning to say simple things, distinguishing one grammatical form from another, getting the syntax. In such a situation there is a long-term relationship in which the informant becomes responsible for maintaining the standards—he has to teach his pupil to speak correctly—and the anthropologist searches, seeks, tries, experiments, plays, explores, and fiddles with everything. He keeps asking the broadest and silliest questions, the simplest and the wildest questions. "Why?" is the paradigm for them all. Why the different ending? Why this word order and not that? Why not that word? Why not say it this way? Why should it sound like that?

Some informants have some ideas about the structure of the language they themselves use. They have some rough and ready notions of the grammar, some generalizations about syntax, some rules of thumb at least about the sounds. The native's model of his own language is not, of course, the same as his language, and neither is it the same model that the anthropologist would construct. But good informants are separated from bad informants by the fact that the former are able to offer useful insights and generalizations, are able to volunteer ideas which are always of some value. A bad informant is only able to say yes or no, right or wrong, and to provide an endless series of "I don't know" answers. But both the good informant and the bad informant speak their language correctly.

The final stages of learning a language in the field are those where the language is actively used as the research tool, where it is the medium through which a wider and wider series of questions can be asked of a wider and wider array of different informants, where facts can be checked quickly and easily, and guesses and hypotheses can be played out against a variety of different natives. Here the vocabulary is expanded from a good working base to fluency, and the field worker can perceive the nuances, allusions, metaphors, the sense of poetry and rhythm, that the first stumbling lessons can never convey.

Although language is one part of culture, and is the key to culture, there is more to any particular culture than just its language; however, language is always the major medium through which communication takes place.

Learning a culture, then, takes place by learning its language, but learning the culture consists of more than just learning the language. Yet learning the culture is just like learning the language.

The relationship with the informant, therefore, is one of the crucial elements in learning the culture. The message has to be conveyed to the informant that the anthropologist wants to know what the informant thinks about the subject, how he sees it, how he understands it, what it means to him, what it is like. In the beginning it is vital that the anthropologist take the position that he knows so little about the subject that he is not even able to frame an intelligent question. The situation is, in fact, just that, whether it is grammatical categories or kinship categories that are being learned. The fundamental position of the anthropologist is that he knows nothing whatever but that he is capable of learning and anxious to learn.

This is the fundamental condition of work with an informant which seeks to locate, define, and describe cultural units or categories, or constructs. The more rigid the frame which the field worker presents to the native, the more likely it is that the informant will behave like a human being and fill *just that* frame for him. The more positive the field worker is that he knows exactly what he wants and just what to look for, the more likely it is that the informant will behave like a decent human being and help him find just exactly that and nothing else. The more clearly the field worker has in mind what he is after, the less likely it is that he will discover what the natives' cultural categories are; how the natives define them, construct them, and manipulate them; or what they mean to the natives.

By the very same token, the fundamental rule of field work is that the informant is seldom if ever wrong, never provides irrelevant data, and is incapable of *pure* fabrication. Short of simple errors of hearing, etc., the integrity of the informant and the integrity of the data are inviolate, and I cannot think of any exceptions to this rule.

It follows that no particular field method is necessarily good or necessarily bad or is to be avoided on principle except, of course, for that which is unethical. Take as an example the loaded question or the leading question. If a survey is to ask one small set of questions of a sample of respondents on a single occasion, the loaded question must be avoided, because it will tend to pull for a particular kind of answer. Since these answers will constitute the entire universe of the data—or very nearly the entire universe of the relevant data—the conclusions will be biased by the way in which the question was asked.

In work with informants where the objective of that work is the location, description, and analysis of cultural units and constructs, a mass of data is collected, consisting of a large number of different kinds and collected over different periods of time. From these data trial hypotheses are formulated, which are then referred back to the data from which they presumably emerged to make them consistent with those data. The hypotheses are then checked against new data as they come in, and particularly against new data that are elicited in such a way as to allow for the disproof of the hypothetical construct. In this situation, then, what is a loaded question in a survey is a perfectly good trial hypothesis. "You people believe in witches, don't you?" is a loaded question. And it is certainly not confirmed or denied by a tally of "yeas" and "nays" from a cross section of the village. There are well-known circumstances where, although in fact it can be demonstrated that the natives believe in witches, not a single native will give an affirmative answer to such a question put in that way.

But then, why ask the question in that way? The answer must be, "Why not?" For any kind of question, put in any way, must be assumed to yield some kind of data of some importance to the task of locating the cultural units and their definitions and meanings, and distinguishing these from regularities of all sorts which are not in themselves the culturally formulated rules.

Yet there is another answer to the "Why not?" that depends on the state of knowledge which the anthropologist has at the time. At first, when there are no data but only an enormous range of hypotheses, almost any data are of direct relevance. Later, as data pile up, many become redundant, affirming and reaffirming the same point. It is at this time that hypotheses about what are and what are not cultural units, their definitions, and the ways in which they are articulated become crucial. And it is at this time that the strategic question that discriminates a good hypothesis from a bad one, a tenable formulation from one which does not work, becomes necessary. Whether the question is loaded or not is of less significance than whether the question can elicit the crucial data for discriminating a false hypothesis from a good one.

Not only does the field worker work in a variety of situations with an informant, asking a variety of different questions in a variety of different ways, exploring, formulating, playing, trying different constructs, but his relationship with the informant becomes a crucial datum in itself. The informant is asked to reflect, to consider, to say why he did or did not do certain things, to remember what others have said or have not said. He tends to become immensely interested in the subject himself, and in a very important sense he becomes the anthropologist. He tries to find answers, understandings, insight, not only to help his anthropologist, but also because he himself has discovered an intellectually or emotionally intriguing question.

It is worth going a step further and listing the kinds and volume of data collected in Chicago and elsewhere on which this book is based.

The largest single block of data comes from interviewing in Chicago between the Fall of 1961 and the end of the Summer of 1963 and consists in over six thousand pages of typed accounts of interviews (not taped transcripts, but as close to verbatim recall as possible) with 102 people, of whom 94 were husband and wife (usually interviewed separately), and the remainder were wives alone (except for one woman and her adult son). In addition, 43 excellent genealogies were taken from the 53 families (the first ten genealogies were not very good since it took some time to learn how to take a genealogy); wedding invitation lists, wedding gift lists, Christmas card lists, cemetery plot listings, funeral books, and a mimeographed family news bulletin completed the data from these 53 families.[2]

In 1965, after I had undertaken some preliminary analysis of that material, Mrs. Linda Wolf conducted interviews with 99 children from the ages of six to 18 and their mothers, on the children's knowledge of their relatives, their view of the meanings and usages of kinship terms, and their definitions of kin and kinship matters. Here children were inter-

---

[2] For a full account of the field work, field methods, and special problems of field work of this sort, see L. Wolf, *Anthropological Interviewing in Chicago*. Mimeographed. American Kinship Projects Monograph #1 (Chicago, 1964).

viewed either once or twice, seldom oftener. These children did not come from families in the first group interviewed.

The Chicago adult informants were middle-class whites, some of whom were Catholic, some Protestant, some Jews; of old Anglo-Saxon, German, Polish, Bohemian, Irish, Greek, Italian, and Jewish ethnic identity.[3]

But this book does not depend on these data alone. It has taken into account materials collected in an earlier study done among the graduate students and faculty of the Department of Social Relations at Harvard University,[4] materials collected informally from friends; neighbors; colleagues; acquaintances; newspaper accounts; newspaper columns; the literature in professional sociology, psychiatry, psychology, and anthropology journals; students' reports; and similarly authentic but unsystematic sources.

The final source of information is, of course, my own personal experience, since I was born and reared in America, am a native speaker of the language, and have lived in America almost all of my life. (I should add that in my own view, I am not a bad informant, although I have worked with better.)

Such a diverse array of sources can, of course, be regarded as a sample in the technical sense that every major segment of the population of the United States is represented in some way. They may be represented di-

---

[3] A series of volumes is now in active preparation which will make much of the Chicago data available in the near future. First, the genealogies of more than 40 families have been coded and put on computer tapes. This material includes name, age, sex, religion, occupation, residence, and the different kinds and frequency of contact with all others on the genealogy for each person listed. Much of the analysis of this material is completed and is being written up for publication at the time of writing. Second, a volume on the field methods used is currently available only in mimeographed draft form. This will be revised for publication. Third, a systematic comparison of the genealogies of parents and their children taken independently of each other will provide the basis for a study of what I have called "peeling." That is, what part of the kin universe of the parents is passed along to the child, what are the losses, what are the processes of this transmission, and so forth. The analysis of this material is nearly complete at this writing. Fourth, a short analysis of the kin knowledge of children is planned. This includes the children's definitions of kin categories, their view of the family and kin universe, and a special analysis of the discrepancies between the child's and his mother's inventory of kin and definitions of the categories. Fifth, a special study of affinal relations, starting with ego's own wedding and subsequent relations based primarily on the interview materials. This should make available the considerable data on wedding invitation lists, gift lists, and subsequent in-law relations now contained in the files. Sixth, a study of funeral and kin behavior at funerals is planned, but analysis of this material has not yet begun. Seventh, a volume on class and kinship is begun but not yet far along. Further studies will be undertaken when these are well along or already published. In the meanwhile, it goes without saying that the files and all of the field materials are available to qualified, interested scholars in Chicago.

[4] See D. M. Schneider and G. C. Homans, "Kinship Terminology and the American Kinship System," *American Anthropologist,* **57** (1955), 1194-1208.

rectly by informants, or indirectly by my reading of the anthropological, sociological, psychological, and psychiatric literature, plus biographies, autobiographies, novels, and discussions with social scientists who have direct knowledge of some subgroup. By "major segment" I mean whites, Negroes, Chinese, Japanese, Greeks, Germans, Bohemians, Irish, Spanish-Americans, Italians, English, Scotch, Poles, Protestants, Catholics, Jews, northeasterners, midwesterners, southerners, far-westerners, upper class, middle class, and lower class. There are certainly many small groups about which I have little direct or indirect information. For instance, although I have read much of the available literature on the Ozark and Appalachian regions, I feel confident only of the most general features of kinship and family life in those regions. But nothing which I say in this book is inconsistent with what I know.

IV.

If this is a sample in the sense that data from every major segment of the population of the United States have had a chance to be taken into account, it is a sample "designed" with reference to the aims of the study. For the aims of the study have to do with cultural constructs, not with frequency distributions. For example, the study aims to show that "dad" is a kinship term, what it means, how it is articulated in a system of kinship terms; it does not aim to show what percentage of persons from which subgroups say that they use the term. Neither does the study aim simply to show that something is or is not present, quite apart from the question of its rate of occurrence. For the question is not whether certain events do or do not occur, but rather that of locating and understanding the cultural units.

The reason for including data from every major segment of the population of the United States is to deal with the question of whether there are as many different kinship systems as there are different subgroups in the United States, or whether there is a single system or some combination of dominant and variant systems. The only way to find out, of course, is to consider the data.

There has never been any doubt that there is variation from group to group in American kinship and family practices. The problem has been to establish its kind and meaning. The sociological, psychological, and psychiatric literature contains many discussions of differences between class, race, ethnic, and religious groups. But these differences are often reported as differences in *rates*. For instance, the high rate of fatherless and husbandless households among lower-class Negroes as compared with middle-class whites is the subject of considerable discussion today, much of which centers on whether this difference in rate can be accounted for in terms of the survival of practices which first took form during the period of American slavery, or as a direct result of economic and social disadvantage.

Unless a difference in rate reflects a difference in cultural form, however, it is not directly relevant to my problem. That is, if the prevalence of matrifocal families in the lower class follows from the fact (for example) that they do not share the same definition of the family which the middle class holds, this is of major importance for this study. But if the prevalence of matrifocal families in the lower class is a direct consequence of economic deprivation, then it is not a different cultural form and it is not a ground for assuming that more than one kind of kinship system occurs in the United States.

Another example, however, puts this matter into a different light. During the field work in Chicago, informants often insisted that their particular ethnic group had distinctive or typical family characteristics which were unlike anything else in America. Since this was a question in which I was interested from the very start of this study, such clues were pursued relentlessly, but tactfully. Over a long period of visits, we asked each informant, "What distinguishes the family of your particular ethnic group?" The answers were illuminating. For the Italians the matter was quite simple; it is not possible to fully understand the Italian family in America until one has understood the Italian mother. For the Irish the matter was equally clear; it is not really possible to understand the Irish family until one has understood the special place of the Irish mother. For the Jews the matter was beyond dispute; it is impossible to fully comprehend the complexities and special qualities of Jewish family life without understanding the Jewish mother. It should be unnecessary to add that the first step in understanding mothers is in understanding the special place which food has in the family, and this leads straight to the problem of cultural units, symbols, the meanings of such units and symbols, and how they articulate.

The situation is in fact much more complex than these simple examples suggest. Almost every conceivable kind of variation seems to be present in American kinship and family practices. Indeed, this statement is no more than the obverse of the often-cited flexibility, adaptability, and fluidity of the system. And this is no more than to reiterate the well-established point that the kinship and family practices of Americans have not stood in the way of economic development as they have in other countries, nor have they impeded the operation of a free labor market or the development of a political bureaucracy based on merit and competence rather than on hereditary and nepotic rights. A system which is so fluid and flexible must be one in which a high degree of variance obtains.

Quite apart from such considerations, direct observation suggests almost immediately that the system is characterized by a very high degree of variance and a corresponding absence of areas of rigidity, and this impression can make the field worker wonder if there is any structure to the system at all!

The question of whether there is a single kinship system or a variety of different kinship systems cannot be studied directly in those terms, for the whole problem is to locate and analyze precisely what kinds of variance occur and at what points they occur. If one kind of variance is a matter of rate and another kind is a matter of basic difference in cultural definition, then each variation itself must be examined to see what kind it is.

Since this is a fundamental point for this book, I must restate it once more. The problem of variance in the American kinship system is one of the major problems of its description and analysis. It is ultimately soluble by distinguishing variance of a cultural order from other kinds, but this solution cannot be imposed on the data prematurely or arbitrarily. The very first task is to locate and establish what kind of variance is involved at every point.

There are four readily discernible kinds of variance in American kinship and family practices. The first and most obvious is that of *rate*. Here, whatever the cultural definitions, rules, and concepts, a variety of forces comes to bear on a given population so that at two different times, or for two different parts of the population, there are differences in the frequency with which a particular item occurs. The word "daddy," for instance, has distinctly feminine connotations in the northeastern part of the United States, not because it is defined as being the proper and appropriate term for women to use, but rather because there is a considerably greater incidence of its use by women than by men. The use of "daddy" by adult men in the south and southwest is at a much higher rate than in the northeast, and as a consequence "daddy" does not have the childish or effeminate connotations in the south and southwest that it does in the northeast. Another example is in the use of "aunt" and "uncle" for the friends of parents. I have the impression that this usage is fading now and was more frequent 25 to 40 years ago. Yet there is no evidence that the definition or meanings of those terms has changed. Certainly there has been change, but it is not at all clear that the change has occurred at the cultural level in the definition of those terms.

A second kind of variance consists in *alternate norms* or *alternate forms*. Here any given person is free to choose which form he uses, and he may use all of the alternatives at one time or another or in one situation or another. Thus "father" and "dad" are alternate terms which Americans can and do use. The same person may use "father" and "dad." Which term he chooses, and when, depends on a variety of considerations, none of which affects the fact that they are equally legitimate alternate forms.

Alternate forms need not be of the *either/or* variety; they also can be of a "some do, some don't" variety. Thus, for instance, whether the cousin's spouse is considered to be a cousin and is called "cousin," and whether the surviving spouse of a mother's brother is or is not considered to be a member of the family can be alternate forms. Both ways are "correct" or can be chosen by different people, or by the same people at different times.

A third kind of variance consists in *variant forms or norms*. Here there is a primary commitment to a particular form by a particular group or segment of the population while other groups use other forms. All agree, however, that no particular form is "right" and the others "wrong." Three terms for marginal, distant kin are examples. The term "wakes-and-weddings relatives" is said to be used primarily by Catholics, "kissin' kin" or "kissin' cousins" primarily by southerners, and "shirt-tail relations" predominantly by midwesterners. Midwesterners who are not Catholic understand what "wakes-and-weddings relatives" are, but do not normally use the term since it is identified as Catholic. They often do not understand what "kissin' cousins" are, unless they have a southern background or have looked into the question, and they identify it as being of the South. Southerners often look puzzled when "shirt-tail relations" are mentioned, for the phrase is foreign to them. They understand it immediately when it is explained, but see it as a mark of northern life with which they are not identified.[5]

A fourth kind of variance, which is really a special case of rate, becomes evident when a question is asked which somehow crosscuts two or more areas of cultural definition or normative regulation and focuses instead on the outcome of strategy decisions which individuals make.

A good example of this is the question of the degree to which kinship relations should be instrumental in aim or content. If informants are asked whether it is better to borrow money from a relative or from a bank the responses range from "A relative! That's what relatives are for!" to "A bank! That's what banks are for!" If the question uses the example of doctors, dentists, or lawyers instead of banks, the answers divide in much the same way. The discussion with informants which follows their presentation of these views dwells on the same considera-

[5] These terms are explained on p. 70 .

tions, but the outcome for any particular person may be one way or the other depending on how the values are calculated. It is precisely because there is no normative stipulation that is culturally defined to contrast instrumental activities against others that the question is open to strategic evaluations. If the question, "Should you help your mother if she is ill?" is asked, there is no division among the answers, no qualifying conditions; the normative prescription is quite clear: "Yes, in any way possible."

The empirical problem is, then, to locate the different areas in which variance occurs, and to identify the type of variance. I do not offer this simple four-part classification of variance as either exhaustive or definitive, but only to indicate that there is an important difference between variation in rate and variation at a cultural level, and that whether one can usefully distinguish different kinship systems within the United States, or whether there is a single system, depends on how the problem of variance is posed and how it is solved. As the second part of this book will make clear, I believe that it is possible, at one distinct level of cultural analysis, to discuss and describe a single kinship system, and at another to define and describe both alternate and variant forms.

V.

I have tried to state as clearly as possible in this Introduction the problem I have chosen and the way in which I have chosen to work with it. This book is intended to be an account of the American kinship system *as a cultural system, as a system of symbols, and not as a "description" at any other level.*

This book is *not* to be understood as an account of what Americans *say* when they talk about kinship and family, although it is based on what Americans say. It is *not* about what Americans *think*, as a rational, conscious, cognitive process, about kinship and family, although it is based in no small part on what Americans say they think about kinship and family. This book should *not* be construed as a *description* of roles and relationships which Americans can be observed actually to undertake in their day-to-day behavior in situations of family life, although it is based on what Americans say they do and on what they have been observed to do.

This book is about symbols, the symbols which are American kinship.

PART ONE

THE DISTINCTIVE FEATURES WHICH DEFINE THE PERSON AS A RELATIVE

CHAPTER TWO

Relatives

What the anthropologist calls kinsmen are called "relatives," "folks, "kin-folk," "people," or "family" by Americans; the possessive pronoun may precede these terms. In different regions and dialects various words may be used, but people from different parts of the country generally understand each other and share the same fundamental definitions even when they do not use the same names for the same cultural categories. I will use the American term "relative" as the very rough equivalent for the anthropologist's term "kinsman," but this is a very rough translation indeed.

The explicit definition which Americans readily provide is that a relative is a person who is related by blood or by marriage. Those related by marriage may be called "in-laws." But the word relative can also be used by Americans in a more restricted sense for blood relatives alone and used in direct opposition to relative by marriage. Thus it may be said, "No, she is not a relative; my wife is an in-law." Or it may equally properly be said, "Yes, she is a relative; she is my wife."

One can begin to discover what a relative is in American culture by considering those terms which are the names for the kinds of relatives— among other things—and which mark the scheme for their classification.

American kinship terms can be divided into two groups. The first group can be called the *basic* terms, the second, *derivative* terms. Derivative terms are made up of a basic term plus a modifier.[1] "Cousin" is an

[1] I take this distinction between basic and derivative terms from W. H. Goodenough, "Yankee Kinship Terminology: A Problem in Componential Analysis," in E. A. Hammel (ed.) "Formal Semantic Analysis," *American Anthropologist*, 67: 5, Part 2 (1965), 259-87.

example of a basic term, "second" a particular modifier. "Second cousin" is an example of a derivative term. "Father" is another example of a basic term, "-in-law" a modifier. "Father-in-law" is an example of a derivative term.

The basic terms are "father," "mother," "brother," "sister," "son," "daughter," "uncle," "aunt," "nephew," "niece," "cousin," "husband," and "wife." The modifiers are "step-" "-in-law," "foster," "great," "grand," "first," "second," etc., "once," "twice," etc., "removed," "half," and "ex-." The "removed" modifier is reserved to "cousin." The "half" modifier is reserved to "brother" and "sister." The "ex-" modifier is reserved to relatives by marriage. "Great" only modifies "father," "mother," "son," and "daughter" when they have first been modified by "grand," as in "great grandfather." "Great" and "grand" do not modify "cousin," "brother," "sister," "husband," or "wife." Otherwise modifiers can be used with any basic term.[2]

The modifiers in this system form two different sets with two different functions. One set of modifiers distinguishes true or blood relatives from those who are not. These are the "step-," "-in-law," and "foster" modifiers along with the "half" modifier which specifies less than a full blood sibling. Thus "father" is a blood relative, "foster brother" is not. "Daughter" is a blood relative, "step-daughter" is not.

The other set of modifiers define the range of the terms as infinite. These are the "great," "grand," "removed," "first," etc., and "ex-" modifiers. That is, the range or extent of the terms is without limit.

There are, therefore, two different kinds of modifiers. One kind, the *restrictive*, sharply divides blood relatives from those in comparable positions who are not blood relatives. The other kind of modifier, the *unrestrictive*, simply states the unrestricted or unlimited range of certain relatives.

One more important point should be noted about the modifiers. The unrestrictive modifiers mark distance, and they mark it in two ways. The

[2] Compare W. H. Goodenough, *op. cit.* For the difference between his view and mine, see footnote, p. 99 , below. It should also be noted that I do not offer this as a definitive or exhaustive list of American kinship terms. "Parent," "child," "sibling," "ancestor," "ancestress," "descendant," "pa," "pappy," "pop," "papa," "ma," "mammy," "mom," "mama," and so forth could all be considered as candidates for such a list, along with terms like "old man," "old woman," "old lady," "governor," and so forth. It is really not possible to assume that there is a finite lexicon or vocabulary of kinship terms without first providing a clear definition of just what a kinship term is and whether this definition is imposed on the data for analytic purposes or whether it is a definition inherent in the culture itself. Since I am not undertaking an analysis of either kinship terms or of terms for kinsmen here, I will reserve these questions for another time. My aim here is simply to use some terms which have kinship meanings as these are defined in American culture, as a way to begin to discover what the American cultural definition of a relative is.

first is by degrees of distance. Thus "first cousin" is closer than "second cousin," "uncle" closer than "great uncle," "great uncle" closer than "great great uncle," and so on. The second way of marking distance is on a simple "in/out" basis. Husband is "in," ex-husband is "out." (But note that "first," "second," etc., as modifiers of "husband" and "wife" do not mark closeness but only succession in time.)

This structure states a substantial part of the definition of what is and what is not a relative. The first criterion, blood or marriage, is central. The two kinds of modifiers are united in their functions; one protects the integrity of the closest blood relatives. The other places relatives in calibrated degrees of distance if they are blood relatives, but either "in" or "out" if they are relatives by marriage.

II.

If a relative is a person related "by blood," what does this mean in American culture?

The blood relationship, as it is defined in American kinship, is formulated in concrete, biogenetic terms. Conception follows a single act of sexual intercourse between a man, as genitor, and a woman, as genetrix. At conception, one-half of the biogenetic substance of which the child is made is contributed by the genetrix, and one-half by the genitor. Thus each person has 100 per cent of this material, but 50 per cent comes from his mother and 50 per cent from his father at the time of his conception, and thereby is his "by birth."

Although a child takes part of the mother's makeup and part of the father's, neither mother nor father shares that makeup with each other. Since a woman is not "made up of" biogenetic material from her husband, she is not his blood relative. But she is the blood relative of her child precisely because the mother and child are both "made up of," in part, the very same material. So, too, are the father and child.

It is believed, in American kinship, that both mother and father give substantially the same kinds and amounts of material to the child, and that the child's whole biogenetic identity or any part of it comes half from the mother, half from the father. It is not believed that the father provides the bone, the mother the flesh, for instance, or that the father provides the intelligence, the mother the appearance.

In American cultural conception, kinship is defined as biogenetic. This definition says that kinship is whatever the biogenetic relationship is. If science discovers new facts about biogenetic relationship, then that is what kinship is and was all along, although it may not have been known at the time.

Hence the real, true, verifiable facts of nature are what the cultural formulation is. And the real, true, objective facts of science (these are the facts of nature too, of course) are that each parent provides one-half of his child's biogenetic constitution.[3]

The relationship which is "real" or "true" or "blood" or "by birth" can never be severed, whatever its legal position. Legal rights may be lost, but the blood relationship cannot be lost. It is culturally defined as being an objective fact of nature, of fundamental significance and capable of having profound effects, and its nature cannot be terminated or changed. It follows that it is never possible to have an ex-father or an ex-mother, an ex-sister or an ex-brother, an ex-son or an ex-daughter. An ex-husband or ex-wife is possible, and so is an ex-mother-in-law. But an ex-mother is not.

It is significant that one may disown a son or a daughter, or one may try to disinherit a child (within the limits set by the laws of the various states). The relationship between parent and child, or between siblings, may be such that the two never see each other, never mention each other's name, never communicate in any way, each acting as if unaware of the other's existence. But to those directly concerned, as to all others who know the facts, the two remain parent and child or sibling to each other. Nothing can really terminate or change the biological relationship which exists between them, and so they remain blood relatives. It is this which makes them parent and child or sibling to each other in American culture.

Two blood relatives are "related" by the fact that they share in some degree the stuff of a particular heredity. Each has a portion of the natural, genetic substance. Their kinship consists in this common possession. If they need to prove their kinship, or to explain it to someone, they may name the intervening blood relatives and locate the ascendent whose blood they have in common. It is said that they can trace their blood *through* certain relatives, that they have "Smith blood in their veins." But their kinship to each other does not depend on intervening relatives, but only on the fact that each has some of the heredity that the other has and both got theirs from a single source.

---

[3] The cultural premise is that the real, true, objective facts of nature about bio-genetic relationships are what kinship "is." But it does not follow that every fact of nature as established by science will automatically and unquestioningly be accepted or assimilated as part of the nature of nature. People may simply deny that a finding of science is true and therefore not accept it as a part of what kinship "is." By the same token, some items in some people's inventories of the real, true, objective facts of nature may be those which scientific authority has long ago shown to be false and untrue but which these Americans nevertheless insist are true. But this should not obscure my point here, which is simply that the cultural definition is that kinship is the biogenetic facts of nature.

Because blood is a "thing" and because it is subdivided with each reproductive step away from a given ancestor, the precise degree to which two persons share common heredity can be calculated, and "distance" can thus be stated in specific quantitative terms.

The unalterable nature of the blood relationship has one more aspect of significance. A blood relationship is a relationship of identity. People who are blood relatives share a common identity, they believe. This is expressed as "being of the same flesh and blood." It is a belief in common biological constitution, and aspects like temperament, build, physiognomy, and habits are noted as signs of this shared biological makeup, this special identity of relatives with each other. Children are said to look like their parents, or to "take after" one or another parent or grandparent; these are confirming signs of the common biological identity. A parent, particularly a mother, may speak of a child as "a part of me."

In sum, the definition of a relative as someone related by blood or marriage is quite explicit in American culture. People speak of it in just those terms, and do so readily when asked. The conception of a child occurs during an act of sexual intercourse, at which time one-half of the biogenetic substance of which the child is formed is contributed by the father, its genitor, and one-half by the mother, its genetrix. The blood relationship is thus a relationship of substance, of shared biogenetic material. The degree to which such material is shared can be measured and is called *distance*. The fact that the relationship of blood cannot be ended or altered and that it is a state of almost mystical commonality and identity is also quite explicit in American culture.

III.

"Relative by marriage" is defined with reference to "relative by blood" in American kinship. The fundamental element which defines a relative by blood is, of course, blood, a substance, a material thing. Its constitution is whatever it is that really is in nature. It is a natural entity. It endures; it cannot be terminated.

Marriage is not a material thing in the same sense as biogenetic heredity is. It is not a "natural thing" in the sense of a material object found in nature. As a state of affairs it is, of course, natural; it has natural concomitants or aspects, but it is not in itself a natural object. It is terminable by death or divorce.

Therefore, where blood is both material and natural, marriage is neither. Where blood endures, marriage is terminable. And since there is no such "thing" as blood of which marriage consists, and since there is no such material which exists free in nature, persons related by marriage are not related "in nature."

If relatives "by marriage" are not related "in nature," how are they related?

Consider the step-, -in-law, and foster relatives. The fundamental fact about these relatives is that they have the role of close relatives without, as informants put it, being "real or blood relatives." A step-mother is a mother who is not a "real" mother, but the person who is now the father's wife. A father-in-law is a father who is not Ego's own father, but his spouse's father. And a foster son is not one's own or real son, but someone whom one is caring for as a son.

It is possible to describe a foster-child's *relationship* to his foster parents, or a step-child's *relationship* (and this is the word which informants themselves use) to his step-parent. This is, in its main outline, a parent–child relationship in the sense that it is a pattern for how interpersonal relations should proceed.

The natural and material basis for the relationship is absent, but relatives of this kind have a relationship in the sense of following a pattern for behavior, a code for conduct.

The classic tragedy of a step-child in Western European folklore, Cinderella for instance, states exactly the nature and also the problem of this relationship. A woman's relationship to her own child is one in which she has an abiding love and loyalty for it; her relationship to her husband's child by his earlier marriage is one in which that child is someone else's child, not hers. What she does for her step-child she does because of her husband's claim on her. Hence, if her husband does not protect his child, she may be cruel to it and favor her own child. This is seen as tragic because a child should have a mother who will mother it, and the parent-child relationship is quite distinct from the blood-tie which underlies it. The cruel step-mother of folklore should rise above the literal definition of her relationship to her step-child, and have the kind of *relationship*—affection, concern, care, and so forth—which a mother has for a child.

When a person is related to a blood relative he is related first by common biogenetic heredity, a *natural substance*, and second, by a *relationship,* a pattern for behavior or a code for conduct. The spouse, on one hand, and the step-, -in-law, and foster- relatives, on the other hand, are related by a *relationship* alone; there is no natural substance aspect to the relationship.

The distinctive feature which defines the order of blood relatives, then, is blood, a natural substance; blood relatives are thus "related by nature." This, I suggest, is a special instance of *the natural order* of things in American culture. The natural order is the way things are in nature. It consists in objects found free in nature. It is "the facts of life" as they really exist.

The feature which alone distinguishes relatives by marriage is their relationship, their pattern for behavior, the code for their conduct. I suggest, this is a special instance of the other general order in American culture, the *order of law*. The order of law is imposed by man and consists of rules and regulations, customs and traditions. It is law in its special sense, where a foster-parent who fails to care properly for a child can be brought to court, and it is law in its most general sense: law and order, custom, the rule of order, the government of action by morality and the self-restraint of human reason. It is a relationship in the sense of being a code or pattern for how action should proceed.

All of the step-, -in-law, and foster relatives fall under the order of law. It is in this sense that a mother-in-law is not a "real" or "true" mother— not a genetrix, that is—but is in the relationship of mother–child to her child's spouse. It is in this sense that a step-mother is not a "real" mother, not the genetrix, but is in a mother–child relationship to her husband's child. The crux of the Cinderella story is precisely that where the "real mother" is related to her child both by law and by nature, the step-mother lacks the "natural" basis for the relationship, and lacking this natural substance she "feels" no love except toward her "own" child and is thus able to cruelly exploit the child related to her *in law* alone.

If there is a relationship in law without a relationship in nature, as in the case of the spouse, step-, -in-law, and foster relatives, can there be a relationship in nature without a relationship in law? Indeed there can and there is. What is called a "natural child" is an example. He is a child born out of wedlock, a child, that is, whose mother and father are not married. He is a "natural child" because in his case his relationship to his parents is by nature alone and not by law as well; he is an "illegitimate" child. Similarly, the "real mother" of a child adopted in infancy, whether legitimate or not, is a relative in nature alone and not in law, and so is the genitor of such a child. Although the child is adopted and has every right and every duty of the blood child, in American belief it remains related to its "true" mother and father, its genitor and genetrix, in nature though not in law.

IV.

In sum, the cultural universe of relatives in American kinship is constructed of elements from two major cultural orders, the *order of nature* and the *order of law*. Relatives in *nature* share heredity. Relatives *in law* are bound only by law or custom, by the code for conduct, by the pattern for behavior. They are relatives by virtue of their *relationship,* not their biogenetic attributes.

Three classes of relatives are constructed from these two elements.

First there is the special class of relatives in nature alone. This class contains the natural or illegitimate child, the genitor or genetrix who is not the adoptive father or mother, and so on. The second class consists of relatives in law alone. This class may be called "by marriage" or it may be called "in law." It contains the husband and wife, the step-, -in-law, foster-, and other such relatives. The third class consists in relatives in nature *and* in law. This class of relatives is called "blood relatives" and contains the "father . . . daughter," "uncle . . . grandaughter," "cousin," sets, and so on.

The second and third classes of relatives can each be divided into two subclasses. The second class, relatives in law alone, consists of the subclass of husband and wife and the remainder, a subclass which contains the step-, -in-law, and foster- relatives, and those for which there are no special lexemes. Husband and wife take basic kinship terms; the others take derivative terms. Husband and wife are the only relatives in law on a par with the closest blood relatives (the "father . . . daughter"

Table I.

Relatives	Nature	Law
(1) In Nature	+	−
(A) Natural child, illegitimate child, natural mother, natural father, etc.		
(2) In Law	−	+
(A) Husband, Wife.		
(B) Step-, -in-law, foster-, etc.°		
(3) By Blood	+	+
(A) Father, mother, brother, sister, son, daughter.		
(B) Uncle, aunt, nephew, niece, grandfather, grandmother, grandson, granddaughter, cousin, first cousin, etc., great grandfather, etc., great grandson, etc.		

° This category includes relatives for whom there are no kinship terms in the usual sense but who can nevertheless properly be counted as, or considered to be, relatives by marriage or in-law. This category of kin, therefore, contains kin without kinship terms. As will be clear from Chapter Five below, the cousin's spouse, the spouse of the nephew or niece of Ego's own spouse, as well as others can occur in this category in American kinship. This follows from the different application of alternate norms *within* the framework set by these categories, and may (or may not) entail the use of alternate kinship terms as well. These points will be developed in Chapter Five.

set). Father and mother are properly also husband and wife. Finally, husband and wife are the only true relatives "by marriage" in one sense of marriage, namely, that sexual relationship between a man and a woman.

The third class also consists of two subclasses. The first consists of the "father . . . daughter" set of relatives, the second of those relatives who take the "uncle . . . granddaughter" and "cousin" terms. The modifier functions symbolize the difference between these subclasses: the first subclass is marked by the restrictive modifiers, the second by the unrestrictive modifiers. That is, the "father . . . daughter" subclass is sharply restricted and distinguished from other kinds or degrees of "father," "mother," etc., while the "uncle . . . granddaughter" and "cousin" sets are infinitely expandable, but each expansion adds a degree of distance. Table I represents this summary.

I have put this summary in terms of the different classes or categories of relatives in American kinship. Yet these categories are built out of two elements, *relationship as natural substance* and *relationship as code for conduct*. Each of these elements derives from or is a special instance of the two major orders which American culture posits the world to be made up of, the *order of nature,* and the *order of law.*

CHAPTER THREE

The Family

"Family" can mean all of one's relatives, but "my family" or "the family" means a unit which contains a husband and wife and their child or children, all of whom are kinds of relatives. "The immediate family" is another way of restricting the all-inclusive scope of "family" from all relatives to certain very close ones.

Family and relatives are thus coordinate categories in American kinship in that they share one of their meanings, though certain of their other meanings diverge. Every member of the family is at the same time a relative, and every relative is, in this sense, a member of the family. The cultural definition of a relative thus applies to members of the family insofar as they are relatives.

But the word "family" is singular, not plural. In its singular form it includes at least three different kinds of family members. The word "relative" in the singular form can mean only one person or one kind of relative. The term "family" thus assembles certain different kinds of relatives into a single cultural unit; this meaning is quite different from the simple plurality of relatives without regard to their kind or to their relationship to each other.

This last point is fundamental. Not only are there different kinds of relatives assembled into a single cultural unit, but these three are in a very special relationship to each other, for they are husband, wife, and child or father, mother, and child to each other.

Since members of the family are kinds of relatives, one may ask if the distinctive features in terms of which relatives are defined and differentiated are not the same as those which define and differentiate the members of the family on one hand, and the family as a cultural unit on the other.

And indeed, this proves to be the case. Sexual intercourse (the act of procreation) is the symbol which provides the distinctive features in terms of which both the members of the family as relatives and the family as a cultural unit are defined and differentiated.

I must pause in this account to make certain points quite explicit and to warn the reader of certain problems which he may encounter in reading this exposition.

First, I am introducing at this point the hypothesis that sexual intercourse is the symbol in terms of which members of the family as relatives and the family as a cultural unit are defined and differentiated in American kinship.

I have already indicated [1] that by a symbol I mean something which stands for or represents something else to which it is not intrinsically or necessarily related. The relationship between symbol and object symbolized is, instead, arbitrary.

If, then, there is an *intrinsic* or *necessary* relationship between sexual intercourse, or any aspect of it, and some cultural aspect of American kinship, then sexual intercourse cannot be regarded as symbolic for that particular aspect of the kinship system.

This is an important problem for this book, but it is best considered after all of the material has been presented, not before. I will, therefore, discuss it in the concluding chapter, but must ask the reader to suspend judgment here with the promise that the time for judgment will come.

It is also important to note that this is presented as a hypothesis about American kinship. Whether it is a fact or not can be established by further research.

The second point which the reader is asked to keep in mind is that in presenting and developing this hypothesis I have been careful that each of my statements is ethnographically true.

The third point is that I am describing the culture of American kinship in very much the same way that I have already described the culture of Yap kinship [2] and that this is very much the same way in which I would describe the kinship system of any society, anywhere. The American reader may find this particularly disconcerting, for at times what he may take as a self-evident fact of life I take as a tenet of his culture.

[1] See the Introduction.

[2] See D. M. Schneider, "Double Descent on Yap," *Journal of the Polynesian Society,* **71** (1962), for example.

Take the purely fictional society, Bongo Bongo. If I wrote of them, "The Bongo Bongo believe that an act of sexual intercourse is impelled by inner forces whose nature cannot be controlled and cannot be understood, forces which compel obedience and cannot be fought," the American reader, fortified by his fine sense of tolerance for the ways and beliefs of others, might take this as an interesting fact and consider its implications for the rest of the kinship system of the Bongo Bongo.

But when I write (as I have written below), "Sexual intercourse is an act which is undertaken and does not just happen," even the most reasonable American reader may wonder whether I am joking or being serious, or trying to inflate a simple and self-evident fact of life into some ponderous anthropological principle.

Whether this is or is not a fact of life at one level—whether in fact human beings can control their sexual impulses as Americans say they can, but the Bongo Bongo say they cannot—is not a relevant question for this book at this point in the description. The question of central relevance is whether this *belief* or this *cultural premise* about the nature of life is a fact which can be observed for Americans. That is, the question which the reader must ask is whether this is or is not an ethnographic fact about American culture.

What I am doing in this book and in this chapter is stating what I have found to be ethnographic facts. I am reporting these facts as accurately as I can and I state them in those places where they are relevant to an understanding of American kinship. If the reader will remember that all of the statements he reads in the following pages are offered as ethnographic facts, or hypotheses about them, there should be no misunderstanding.

Finally, the concept of "distinctive features" is one of the fundamental concepts of this book. I have used it both in the title to this Part of the book ("The Distinctive Features Which Define the Person as a Relative") and as a major analytic device in this chapter. I have taken this concept directly from linguistics, and although I have tried to use it as precisely here as it is used there, this has not always been easy. Jakobson and Halle say "Each distinctive feature involves a choice between two terms of an opposition that displays a specific differential property, diverging from the properties of all other oppositions." [3] But the reader may prefer to follow my discussion rather than attempt to fathom this highly condensed definition. Or he should go to Jakobson and Halle for a full and clear discussion in a linguistic context.

I now resume the ethnographic account of the cultural unit, "the

[3] R. Jakobson and M. Halle, *Fundamentals of Language* (The Hague: Mouton & Co., 1965), p. 4.

family," in American kinship. First I will show that the family is defined by American culture as a "natural" unit which is "based on the facts of nature." I then will order certain ethnographic facts which lead to the hypothesis which I have just stated, that is, that the fact of nature which serves as the symbol in terms of which members of the family are defined and differentiated and in terms of which each member of the family's proper mode of conduct is defined is that of sexual intercourse.

II.

"The family" is a cultural unit which contains a husband and wife who are the mother and father of their child or children.

One may say, "I have no family," and mean that perhaps one is not married, and has no spouse or child, or that one's parents are no longer alive. Or, one may point to certain persons and say of them, "This is my family," or "I would like you to meet my family." One may also say, "I have no family," meaning that one is separated from one's spouse and therefore not living with a spouse and children.

A married couple without children does not quite make a family. Neither do a married woman and her children without a husband nor a married man and his children without a wife. For the married couple without children, one may say, "They have no family," or, "Their family has not arrived yet," if they are very young. "Family" here means that the addition of children to the married couple will complete the unit and will bring about that state. And of course one may say of an older couple, "Their family has all grown up and is married; each has a family of his own now."

This last example makes clear another condition which is part of the definition of the family in American kinship. The family, to be a family, must live together. So for parents whose children are grown up and married, the saying is that those children "have families of their own," implying that one's family is where one lives and that it is not possible to be a member of two families (in this sense) at one time. A family where the children have grown up and all have families of their own is one which has broken up and dispersed; its members have gone their independent ways, as they should, of course. Yet this remains a family in the first sense of the term which means parents and children, quite apart from how grown-up they are or where they may be living. It is the second sense that concerns me now, which is that the family is a unit which lives together; if it does not, it is not a family in this particular meaning of the term.

I said that a woman and her children, or a man and his children, do not quite constitute a family. The family is incomplete, for it lacks a member. This might be because the missing member is dead or separated or divorced. The remaining members do not constitute a whole family. But note that whether it is a spouse who is missing because of death, separation, or divorce, or whether it is the children who are missing because they have grown up and "have families of their own" does not really matter. The family is "broken up" in each case because they are not living together.

If a man leaves his wife, it is sometimes said, "He walked out on her and left her alone with the children." Or a woman may desert her husband, "leaving him alone with the children." If one's children grow up and marry, it is also said that "they are alone now that their children are grown-up and off on their own." In each case being "alone" means that the whole unit is not living together, and it is the notion of living together which is decisive to this meaning of the family.

When a couple have a child and are then divorced, and each remarries and establishes a new family, the custody of the child may be divided between them. Perhaps the child lives for half of the time with one parent and the other half of the time with the other. In a situation of this sort the child may have two families, one through his mother and step-father, one through his father and step-mother. He is living together with them if he lives with each one a part of the time, or even if he is in fact away at school most of the time. People may say that the child really has no family at all, for the two half-time arrangements are thought to be much less than one full-time arrangement. Whether he lives with his mother and step-father half of the time, or whether he lives at a boarding school most of the time, it is really the question of custody and responsibility that is important. But perhaps, in a technical sense, the child of divorced parents has two families and not just one, if each parent has established a new family which is living together, and custody is shared.

The state of a family's well-being is described in terms of living together, too. If husband and wife have been having marital difficulties, the critical question may be whether or not they are still living together. If they are, the outlook may not be considered so grave as if they are no longer living together. Living together can also be used as a euphemism for sexual intercourse, for it implies an intimacy between a man and woman that precludes any other interpretation.

Informants describe the family as consisting of husband, wife, and their children who live together as a natural unit. The family is formed according to the laws of nature and it lives by rules which are regarded by Americans as self-evidently natural.

So Americans are not really surprised when they hear that this same sort of arrangement is found among some animals and birds and even fish. It seems quite natural for a pair to live together, to mate, to have a place of their own with their offspring, to protect that place and their offspring, and to share the tasks of keeping the place and rearing the offspring.

It is only natural, in the American view, that the various tasks of protecting the home, of providing the necessities of life, of giving care and instruction to the young, and so forth, be divided according to the natural talents, aptitudes, and endowments of those involved. Certain of these tasks naturally fall to men, certain to women, and certain ways are natural to children because of their age.

Women bear children, nurse them, and care for them. This, according to the definition of American culture, is part of women's nature. They can do these things by virtue of their natural endowment, though there is a great deal that they must learn as well. They may learn these things from their mothers, doctors, books, or elsewhere but these sources explain the things that need to be done and how best to do them naturally.

Men do not bear children, nor can they nurse them from their own bodies. The cultural premise is that they are not naturally endowed with ways of sensing infants' needs. But there are many things which a man can do if he cares to learn. What a woman can do naturally, it is sometimes said in America, a man can learn—albeit slowly and not always with the smooth skill which a woman would exhibit.

The American cultural premise is that the newborn child is quite helpless and requires a great deal of care and protection for its survival. Except for some instincts and reflexes which keep it breathing, sucking, crying, learning, and so on, things have to be done for and to the child. Adults, the child's parents, are old enough and know enough about what to do. This is the basis for the authority of the parents over the child, and for the fact that the relationship between child and parent is not equal. It is one in which the adult has authority based on knowledge and experience—age, in a word—one in which the authority of the adult is supported, if necessary, by force, which also rests on self-evident physical differences between parent and child.

In one of its fundamental senses, then, nature alone does constitute the family, and the natural roles of husband, wife, father, mother, and child define the members of the family. This is the sense in which Americans see a family when animals mate and rear their young in a place which they occupy and protect—their nest, their cave, their home. It is in this sense that the distinctive features or the defining elements of the family posit the mated pair who rear their young in a place of their own.

Yet once this is said, there is a marked shift in informants' statements. At one level of contrast it is the family as a natural unit and the natural roles of the members of the family that is stressed. At the very next level there is something more to the roles of husband, wife, father, mother, and child than merely those parts required by their natural endowments and the natural differences between them. This "something more" is defined as *additions* to the natural endowments, as *accretions* to the natural differences, as *implementation* of the innate tendencies.

Informants often phrase this as being "based on." The authority of the father, for instance, is said by informants to be "based on" the fact that he is male, that he is older, that his experience is wider, that by virtue of his size and his sex he has the right to set the proper course of action for the members of his family and to expect compliance with it.

"Based on" means that something is added to the natural facts of age and sex. "Older" means that added to chronological age is the measure of wisdom which experience supposedly brings. "Being a man" means that added to the specific matter of having certain genital organs, there is the possession of qualities which women are presumed to lack. To speak of "the man of the house" or "the man of the family" or "who wears the pants" is to speak of one who is naturally best able to take authority and responsibility for the family, not just someone with male genitalia and a stipulated number of years on earth.

This increment, what is "based on" the natural elements, is said to be the outcome of the addition of human reason to the natural state of affairs.

Human reason does two things. First, though it builds on a natural base, it creates something additional, something more than what nature alone produces.

Second, human reason selects only part of nature on which to build. This is because nature itself is composed of two distinct parts. One is good, the other bad; one is human, the other animal. Human reason selects the good part of nature to build on; it can set goals and select paths, judge right from wrong, and tell good from bad.

The family, in American kinship, is defined as a natural unit based on the facts of nature. In American culture, this means that only certain of the facts of nature are selected, that they are altered, and that they are built upon or added to. This selection, alteration, and addition all come about through the application of human reason to the state of nature.

The cultural construct of the family in American kinship thus derives from the two orders of the world: the order of nature on the one hand,

and the order of law, the rule of reason, the human as distinct from the animal, on the other hand.

What is human is, of course, a part of nature, yet it is a very special part. That role which is so natural as to have nothing in the way of reason, nothing in the way of human value, nothing of culture, is only natural in the sense of being very close to animal. So a man or woman who is interested in copulation alone cannot be regarded as a good husband or wife. But by the very same token, the role which is so far removed from nature, so highly reasoned, and so far cultivated as to lack any natural element is said to be unnatural. And by this measure, a man or woman wholly uninterested in copulation cannot be regarded as a good husband or wife.

The family, as a construct of American culture, thus resolves the radical opposition between nature and human reason, bringing these two together into a workable, livable, human arrangement.

III.

The fact of nature on which the cultural construct of the family is based is, as I have already suggested, that of sexual intercourse. This figure provides all of the central symbols of American kinship.

It will be convenient to this discussion to begin with the definition of a relative, for each member of the family is a relative and I have already presented much of that ethnographic material.

A relative is a person who is related by blood or marriage. Relatives by blood are linked by *material* substance; husband and wife are linked by *law*. Relatives by blood are related in an entirely *objective* way; husband and wife are linked *subjectively*. Blood is a *permanent* tie; marriage can be *terminated*. All of the statements which open the oppositions derive from the order of nature; those which close them derive from the order of law.

A relationship by blood is involuntary in two distinctly different ways. The first is that a blood relationship is not a matter of human volition. It is part of the natural order and therefore follows the laws of nature and not the laws of man. Marriage, on the other hand, is defined and created by the laws of man, which are of human invention and therefore, in that special sense, are a matter of volition.

In a second sense, blood relationships are involuntary because a man cannot choose who his blood relatives will be. He is born with them and they become his by birth. Since they are permanent, there is nothing that he can do about it. But marriage is not only an institution invented by man; it is an active step which a particular person must take. It is a step which is *taken* and does not just happen.

Blood is a matter of birth, birth a matter of procreation, and procreation a matter of sexual intercourse. Sexual intercourse is an act which is undertaken and does not just happen. Yet as an act, it is natural. Its outcome is conception, which is followed by birth, and these are natural, too.

Sexual intercourse as an act of procreation creates the blood relationship of parent and child and makes genitor and genetrix out of husband and wife. But it is an act which is exclusive to and distinctive of the husband–wife relationship: sexual intercourse is legitimate and proper only between husband and wife and each has the exclusive right to the sexual activity of the other.[4] These are the tenets of American culture.

Sexual intercourse is an act in which and through which love is expressed; it is often called "making love," and love is an explicit cultural symbol in American kinship.

This was expressed by one of our informants—an elderly lady—as follows: We asked her to list all of her relatives and after she had been listing them for a time she slowed down and stopped. She was then asked: "I notice that you did not mention your husband. Do you consider him a relative?" To which she gave the thoughtful reply: "My husband? A lover, Yes! A relative, No!"

There are two kinds of love in American kinship, which, although not explicitly named, are clearly defined and distinguished. One I will call *conjugal* love. It is erotic, having the sexual act as its concrete embodiment. This is the relationship between husband and wife. The other kind of love I will call *cognatic*. The blood relationship, the identity of natural substance and heredity which obtains for parent and child is its symbolic expression.

Cognatic love has nothing erotic about it. In fact, it is believed that infants and children do not have sexual or erotic feelings and that such feelings only mature late among human beings, at around the time of adolescence. An infant's relationship to its mother's breast is therefore wholly nonerotic. Whatever gratification a mother may feel nursing her child is defined as purely cognatic in character. So an infant or child can be hugged and kissed and fondled in ways that might be erotic were the

4 Sexual intercourse between persons who are not married is fornication and improper; between persons who are married but not to each other is adultery and wrong; between blood relatives is incest and prohibited; between persons of the same sex is homosexuality and wrong; with animals is sodomy and prohibited; with one's self is masturbation and wrong; and with parts of the body other than the genitalia themselves is wrong. All of these are defined as "unnatural sex acts" and are morally, and in some cases, legally, wrong in American culture.

object other than an infant. A child is innocent of carnal knowledge both because it is said to be unable physically to experience erotic love, but also because it does not know the meaning of erotic love. The frequency with which a child is appropriately designated as "it," without reference to its sex, is a facet of this. Since the essence of erotic love is genital contact, and since it is believed that the child is too young to have or feel erotic impulses or sensations, its genitals are defined as organs of excretion.

The kiss is an expression of love. The direct kiss on the lips is erotic, and this can be a euphemism for sexual intercourse in certain contexts. But the kiss on the brow or cheek is a cognatic statement. Where lovers or husband and wife may kiss on the lips, parents and children kiss on the brow or cheek. The ceremonial kiss of a visiting relative bestowed on a child is not often mistaken for an erotic act. It affirms cognatic love, and for the child to reject such a kiss is no trivial matter.

The conjugal love of husband and wife is the opposite of the cognatic love of parent, child, and sibling. One is the union of opposites, the other is the unity which identities have, the sharing of biogenetic substance. The mother's identity with her child is further reiterated by the fact that the child is born of her body and that it is nurtured and nourished there before it is born, as well as being nourished from it after the child is born. This restates again and again that the two are of a common substance.

It is the symbol of love which links conjugal and cognatic love together and relates them both to and through the symbol of sexual intercourse. Love in the sense of sexual intercourse is a natural act with natural consequences according to its cultural definition. And love in the sense of sexual intercourse at the same time stands for unity.

As a symbol of unity, or oneness, love is the union of the flesh, of opposites, male and female, man and woman. The unity of opposites is not only affirmed in the embrace, but also in the outcome of that union, the unity of blood, the child. For the child brings together and unifies in one person the different biogenetic substances of both parents. The child thus affirms the oneness or unity of blood with each of his parents; this is a substantive affirmation of the unity of the child with each of his parents and with his siblings by those parents. At the same time, that unity or identity of flesh and blood, that oneness of material, stands for the unity of cognatic love.

Both love and sexual intercourse turn on two distinct elements. One is the unification of opposites. The other is the separation of unities.

Male and female, the opposites, are united in sexual intercourse as husband and wife. Their different biogenetic substances are united in the child conceived of that union and their relationship to each other is re-affirmed not only as husband and wife to each other, but as parents of their child, father and mother to the same offspring.

But what was one must become two. The child is born of its parents and is separated from them physically through its birth. It is this which differentiates parent from child, father and mother from son and daughter. The separation which begins with the act of birth continues until the child grows up and leaves its family to marry and found its own family.

Incest, which is the gravest wrong, consists in unifying what is one to begin with by the device for unifying opposites, and of failing to separate what was one into two, thereby directly inverting in one stroke both sides of the formula, that only different things can be united by sexual intercourse and only united things made different.

The symbol of love bridges these two different elements. It is love which unites the opposites of male and female, and it is love which preserves the unity of the differentiated and further differentiating parents and their children, as well as the child from his siblings. The one is conjugal love, marked by an erotic component; the other is cognatic love, wholly without erotic aspect; but both are love, which is unifying. And love is what American kinship is all about.

One of our informants, a twelve-year-old girl, was asked, "What's your definition of a relative?" and replied, "Someone who you generally love, who's kind to you, and who in some way is related to you by blood like a daughter or something." There is really nothing more that can be added to her statement. It sums the matter up perfectly.

All of the significant symbols of American kinship are contained within the figure of sexual intercourse, itself a symbol, of course. The figure is formulated in American culture as a biological entity and a natural act. Yet throughout, each element which is culturally defined as natural is at the same time augmented and elaborated, built upon and informed by the rule of human reason, embodied in law and in morality.

IV.

What about those other facts of nature which seem to have a very important place in the definition of the family and in the differentiation of its members, facts such as the differences between the sexes? Is this not a fact of nature on which the family is based?

The answer to this very general question is both Yes and No. Two different domains of sex are distinguished in American culture. One is that of sexual attributes, and the other is that of sexual intercourse. Sexual intercourse is the symbol which provides the distinctive features or the elements in terms of which the family is defined. Sexual attributes, on the other hand, constitute facts of nature of great importance to the family but on a quite different cultural level than that of the distinctive features.

In American culture, the definition of what makes a person male or female is the kind of sexual organs he has. Although a child is not a man or a woman until it is sexually mature, its identity as a male or female is established at birth by its genitals.

There are, in addition, certain characteristics which are indicators of sex identity. Men have facial hair and are said to have hair on their chests, but women do not. Temperamental differences are held to correlate with the differences in sexual organs. Men have an active, women a passive quality, it is said. Men have greater physical strength and stamina than women. Men are said to have mechanical aptitudes that women lack. Women have nurturant qualities which men lack. Men tend toward an aggressive disposition said to be absent in women.

The different qualities of maleness and femaleness are said by informants to fit men and women for different kinds of activities and occupations. Men's active, aggressive qualities, their strength and stamina, are said to make them particularly good hunters and soldiers and to fit them for positions of authority, especially where women and children are concerned. Women are presumed to be nurturant and passive in ways that make them particularly good at teaching school, nursing, food preparation, and homemaking. Men's mechanical aptitudes are said to make them good at working with machines—at designing, building, and repairing them—in ways which women cannot match.

In American culture, sex-role occurs in a context which further selects, modifies, or emphasizes some of its special aspects. A man is a policeman, a repairman, a clerk, or a soldier. A woman may be a nurse, a schoolteacher, a cook, or a chambermaid. The attributes of the sex-role have different values in each of these cases. Not only is the policeman a man, but he is a man relying on his strength and fortitude in a context of maintaining law and order and preventing crime. The same qualities of maleness in a soldier are not matters of law and order at all, but are defined by the nature of war. And the repairman using the qualities of his masculinity to tend machines finds his sex-role spelled out in a context of machinery and mechanical aptitudes which may or may not have anything to do with law and order or war, but which focus instead on the efficient operation of the machinery.

The same is true for the family. Wife, mother, daughter, and sister are female; husband, father, son, and brother are male. It is often said that wives and mothers are the proper members of the family to cook, keep house, and care for children, and husbands and fathers are the proper members of the family to go out to work, earn the living, be in charge of the family, and have authority.

But a very fundamental and important piece of evidence comes up at this point if such statements are discussed with good informants. They say—sometimes in so many words, sometimes in the course of the discussion but without putting it in just these words—that if wives and mothers are the proper members of the family to cook and keep house, this is *not* because they are wives and mothers, but because they are *women*. And if husbands and fathers are the members of the family who should go out and earn the living, who should be in charge of the family, this is because they are *men* and *not* because they are husbands and fathers.

Informants sometimes use phrases like "the man of the house" when speaking of the husband–father as the person who has authority; or "the lady of the house" when speaking of the wife–mother as the person who tends to the meals and the comfort of the home. Phrases like "a woman's work is never done" are used to describe the work a wife and mother does. Not because the work is wife's work or mother's work, but because that is woman's work. Sometimes Americans speak of fixing the furnace or controlling the family finances as "a man's job," not because fixing the furnace or finances are distinctively paternal or husbandly activities but because fathers and husbands are men.

This means that there are two distinct cultural units that are easily confused but must be kept separate. A person's action as a man is defined in ways which are different from the definition of his action as a father or husband. The same person can be both a woman and a wife; "work" in "a woman's work is never done" is part of her definition as a woman and not as a wife.

Yet the fact remains that by cultural definition "father" is a male and cannot be female, "mother" is a female and cannot be male, "husband" is male, and "wife" is female. How, then, are we to understand this fact?

What *defines* the cultural units of husband and wife or father and mother? It is demonstrably not their sex. For informants and direct observation confirm that being a man is the necessary but not sufficient condition for being a husband and father. Though all husbands and fathers are men, many men are neither husbands nor fathers.

Similarly, the defining element or the distinctive feature of the cultural categories of wife and mother is not that of being female. There are many kinds of females who are neither wives nor mothers, though no wife or mother is not also female.

The distinction I am drawing here between a defining element or distinctive feature and all other features is nicely illustrated by the area of sex-role definition which I have been describing. As I have said, there are two culturally defined categories, male and female. Male has one kind of genitalia, female another. Male has facial hair, female does not. Male is active and aggressive, female passive.

Consider, now, these three features—genitals, facial hair, and activity. Which is the distinctive feature? From the fact that the bearded lady of the circus is counted as a lady it follows that facial hair is not the distinctive feature. From the fact that an aggressive woman can be criticized for being "too masculine" but remains an aggressive *woman* it follows that activity is not the distinctive feature of sex-role. But if a person dresses in female clothing, lacks facial hair, is passive, but has male genitals, that person is classed as male. Genitals, therefore, are the distinctive feature in terms of which sex-role is defined.

The distinctive features which define the members of the family and differentiate them from each other and which at the same time define the family as a unit and distinguish it from all other cultural units are those which are contained in the symbol sexual intercourse. Father is the genitor, mother the genetrix of the child which is their offspring. Husband and wife are in sexual relationship and theirs is the only legitimate and proper sexual relationship. Husband and wife are lovers and the child is the product of their love as well as the object of their love; it is in this sense that there are two kinds of love which define family relationships, one conjugal and the other cognatic, and it is in this sense that love is a synonym for sexual intercourse.

Yet at another level entirely, certain ethnographic facts remain and constitute a fundamental part of the American kinship system. Wife, mother, sister, and daughter are female; husband, father, brother, and son are male. Unless one of them is a step-relative, wife, mother, husband, and father are all older than sister, daughter, brother, and son. Also, the norms which define what is right and proper for a lower-class father are different from those for a middle-class father.

Quite apart from the distinctive features that define the family and its members, each member is *also* a person and as a person is constructed out of not one, but many different elements, each drawn from many different sources.

Wife and mother are the same person in American kinship, whatever other differences there are between the two, and husband and father are also the same person. But wife and daughter must be different persons, as must husband and son. A man may be both a son and a brother, a woman both a daughter and a sister. But the idea that the wife in the family could be one person, the mother quite another is unthinkable in American kinship.

I must stop the description of the relative as a person at this point. This concept is a major part of the American kinship system, but Part One of this book is exclusively concerned with the distinctive features of the members of the family as relatives and with the family as a unit. Here it is fundamental to distinguish between the father as a father and as a man, the mother as a mother and as a woman, etc. Part Two is reserved for the description of the relative as a person and of the family as a group of persons. It is at that point that the fact that the father is at the same time a man, perhaps of middle class, possibly Protestant, and so on becomes relevant.

v.

The figure of sexual intercourse contains the central symbols of American kinship, each element in it set in relation to the others and to the whole. The image of the family replicates that figure, but adds to its meaning significantly.

Sexual intercourse states and defines the elements of kinship and the relations of those elements to each other. The family also states the elements and their relation to each other, but it is at the same time a paradigm for how family or kinship relations should be conducted, and to what end. Yet the nature of the constituent elements, their definition, their postulation as natural and cultural entities (that is, selected by human reason and formed by man's law from the facts of nature), and their relations to each other as stated in the figure of sexual intercourse are at the same time symbols in the pattern for the proper conduct of kinship as it is stated in the paradigm of the family.

Although the pattern stating how kinship should be conducted applies to the family as a whole, it also informs all kinds of family relations and all parts of the family. Members of the family are distinguished from each other *within* the family. They are not distinguished *from* the family or *against* the family. Whatever other meanings husband, wife, mother, father, son, daughter, brother, and sister may have, they share that set of meanings defined for the family because they are themselves defined as members of the family, and the family is defined as made up of them. The family, therefore, stands for how kinship should be conducted and, because they are members of the family, it stands at the same time for how the husband and wife and their children should conduct themselves.

For example, Americans often hold the family responsible for the troubles which children get into, juvenile delinquency, the high divorce rate, marital infidelity, alcoholism, crime, poverty, drug addiction, and countless other disturbing events. It is also sometimes said, though perhaps less often, that the family is responsible for some commendable state of affairs such as the low rate of juvenile delinquency of some ethnic or religious group.

At first sight it seems absurd either to blame or credit "the family," because the theory which these same Americans hold is that a child's delinquency is due to the negligence or irresponsibility of the parents, and that if the parents did their job properly, these things would not happen. It is the parents, therefore, who are to blame, and not "the family" at all. In the same way, if divorce occurs or does not occur when it should occur, it seems hard to understand why "the family" as a whole should be held accountable when presumably it is the husband and wife who are responsible and not the children.

Why, then, should "the family" be held accountable? In what sense is the word used in such statements?

"The family" stands for each member and for all members of the family, for how each member of the family should behave, and for how family relations should be conducted by whoever is conducting them. If "the family" were right, then the child would not be delinquent, the marriage would be stable, and so on. This means that if everyone in the family behaved according to the proper standards for family life, all would be well.

The family as a symbol is a pattern for how kinship relations should be conducted; the opposition between "home" and "work" defines these meanings quite clearly and states them in terms of the features which are distinctive to each and opposed to the other.

I have said that a family lives together, and where it lives is "home." The difference between a house and a home is celebrated in song, story, and proverb. A house is where a family lives: the way in which it lives there can make it into a home. To "feel at home" is opposed to all other states, which imply a sense of being alien. One can hire a housekeeper, a person who manages the different tasks of keeping house, but a home-maker makes a house into a home and no amount of money (it is said) can buy this.

One of the most fundamental and yet specific ways in which kinship is distinguished from all other kinds of relations is in the physical separation of work and home. This separation is seen most vividly in those special cases where, for some reason, work and home are in very close physical proximity. Where a shop is run by a family with living quarters in the rear, or upstairs, or where a doctor or lawyer has consulting rooms in his house or apartment, the line between the two is very sharply drawn. It may be nothing but a curtain or a door, but the boundary is treated with the utmost respect.

The segregation of culturally distinct domains by physical location is explicit in such phrases as: "A place for everything and everything in its place" and "There is a time and place for everything." More specifically relevant here is the statement: "A man's home is his castle," not only as an affirmation of the privacy of the home, but also as a sign that there should be no intrusion of either domain by the other. The physical separation of the places marks the sharp separation of the domains themselves.

Work, like home, is both a place and an activity. Otherwise, work and home are different in every significant way. Different things are done at home and at work, toward different ends and in different ways by different people.

Work is productive, its outcome a product of some kind. Whether this is an object like a pair of shoes, a service like legal counsel, or entertainment like a theater does not matter. Work has an objective or goal which is clear, explicit, and unitary. One can ask of any place of work: "What is done there?" and the answer given is the objective of that form of work. Perhaps it is a factory: "They make shoes." Perhaps it is a particular person in the factory: "He stitches soles."

Home has no such specific, explicit, unitary objective or goal. The outcome of home is not a single product, a specific form of entertainment, or a special service.

Home is not kept for money and, of those things related to home and family, it is said that there are some things that money can't buy! The formula in regard to work is exactly reversed at home: What is done is done for love, not for money! And it is love, of course, that money can't buy.

Americans say that you can pick your friends but not your relatives: you are born with them. You can also pick the person who does a job for you and if he fails to do the job properly you can fire him and get someone else to do it. Ex-friends and ex-job holders are part of the cast of characters in American life.

But there are no ex-fathers, ex-mothers, ex-brothers or ex-sisters, ex-sons or ex-daughters. Neither can they be picked for the job. One is born with them. One may be lucky or not so lucky, but there are no refunds or exchanges or second chances where blood relatives are concerned. One takes what one gets.

The standards which apply to an employee are different from those which apply to relatives. On a job, the question is whether there is technical competence and the performance standards are set by the technical nature of the job. It may be output measured by the number of items manufactured or how much material is moved in a given time. The nature of the work itself states what is to be done; standards are set and performance can then be matched against those standards. But all of this is within the framework of some set of mechanical, impersonal considerations.

With relatives, it is who one is and not how he does or what he does that counts. With employees, at work, it is what one does and how he does it that counts. Who he is is not supposed to really matter. With relatives, at home, with the family, it is a question of how the other person is related that matters. At work, on the job, it does not matter how the person got the job, but how he does the job.

I do not mean that a mother who does a bad job of it is above reproach or beyond criticism. I mean that she cannot lose her position as mother no matter how badly she does it. She may lose custody of the child, but she remains its mother.

Husband and wife are not blood relatives to each other. But neither are they employees. One does not fire a spouse, but a marriage can be ended by divorce or annulment under certain conditions. An ex-wife or an ex-husband can be a good friend and later, perhaps, even an ex-friend as well.

But the standards which apply to employees simply do not apply to a spouse. There is no technical job description for a husband or a wife in which an output of some product like clean diapers or an earning capacity of so much per week can be set for a spouse of a given age, sex, or standard of quality. One can certainly compare spouses, and one does, in terms of whether they are good cooks or not, helpful husbands, handy around the house, or good breadwinners. One spouse may be kind, another mean. A wife may be lazy or hardworking, but even if a spouse rates low on every measure of competence or productivity which can be applied, from the output of clean shirts per week to the number of fond endearments issued each month, this *in itself* is not proper or sufficient grounds for terminating a marriage. An employee is fired for poor performance according to technical standards. A spouse is not divorced for poor performance as measured by technical standards applied to a job. Neither can a spouse be divorced or a marriage annulled for failure to do a specific job *as a job*.

Marriage is "in sickness and in health, for better or for worse, until death do us part." It is for keeps, forever, just as the stories about the Prince and the Princess have it, where they get married and live happily ever after.

Marriage is not a job, and a spouse cannot be fired like an incompetent mechanic or an inefficient seamstress. That a spouse can be divorced, a marriage annulled, depends on the fact that *the relationship* can be terminated, and this depends on the fact that it is a relationship in law, but not one of substance.

Recreation stands midway between home and work and combines the major symbolic features of both. Like everything else in American culture, it has its own special place, for one takes a vacation by going away, to a place which is neither work nor home. Where work is for money and home is for love, recreation is for gratification, to restore, to recreate. One does what one likes to do on vacation. If one likes to fish or hunt or go to the seashore or just lie about and relax, then that is the sort of thing to do on a vacation.

A vacation is productive—of many fish, or animals killed, or pictures painted, or books read—not because these things are productive for money, but because that is what one likes to do.

Perhaps one can go to a resort or a hotel-and-nightlife place for a vacation. There one finds all the comforts of home but none of its restrictions. A room is private, the bed is private, the bath is private, but the meals may be taken in a dining room of some size. At one's own table certainly, with one's family or whoever is sharing the recreation. But the person on vacation does not prepare the meals or tend to the housekeeping chores. One pays for such services, and some people are in the business (at work) of providing vacations or recreation for others. The success of the vacation is measured not by its cost, but by the ratio of gratification to cost. "Was it worth it? Did you have a good time?" are the questions asked.

The set of features which distinguishes home and work is one expression of the general paradigm for how kinship relations should be conducted and to what end. These features form a closely interconnected cluster.

The contrast between love and money in American culture summarizes this cluster of distinctive features. Money is material, it is power, it is impersonal and unqualified by considerations of sentiment or morality. Relations of work, centering on money, are of a temporary, transitory sort. They are contingent, depending entirely on the specific goal—money. Money gives a person power, that is, advantage over other people. That it also comes between people is the subject of a vast literature. Money measures whether or not the outcome of work, a product or service of some kind, has value and if it has, how much.

Love is not material. It is highly personal and is beset with qualifications and considerations of sentiment and morality. Love brings different things together and unifies them. The outcome of love is not a material product for sale, and the relations of love have an enduring quality which is contrary to the contingent quality of work. Indeed, its goal or value lies in its enduring qualities, among others.

But the opposition between money and love is not simply that money is material and love is not. Money is material, but love is *spiritual*. The spiritual quality of love is closely linked with the fact that in love it is personal considerations which are the crucial ones. Personal considerations are a question of who it is, not of how well they perform their task or how efficient they are. Love is a relationship between persons. Morality and sentiment in turn are the essence of the spiritual quality of love, for they transcend small and petty considerations of private gain or advantage or mere gratification. And as money is material, its quality is of the moment. It is destructible and its transitory nature is paramount. But love is spiritual, enduring, and indestructible. And so relations of money have narrow, specific ends and the relations are not only transient, but also destructive of spiritual values.

VI.

The symbols of American kinship are many and varied and run a wide gamut. But they are all essentially redundant in one of their aspects, while other aspects vary with different contexts and domains.

The symbols of American kinship consist of the unity of flesh and blood, in the fact that the child looks like the parents or takes after a grandparent, and in the affirmation that blood is thicker than water—one meaning of this is reiterated in the statement: "A house is not a home." The symbols of American kinship affirm that the union of a husband and wife is a spiritual union as it is a union of the flesh, that it is a personal union, and that out of that union a new person is formed. The word for such a spiritual union is love. Love brings opposites together into a single unit, while it holds together those things which are moving apart—the child and its parents, or brothers and sisters growing up, finding mates of their own, and founding their own families. The symbols of American kinship consist of motherly love and brotherly love and conjugal love and paternal love, and filial feelings of loyalty and respect. Marriage is for love, and forever, "through thick or thin, for better or for worse, till death do us part." It may *be* fun but it is not *for* fun.

But what, then, do all of these varied and different symbols mean? What do they tell people to do? How should they act? What is the paradigm for how kinship or family relations are to be conducted? To what end?

Certain specific actions are either required or explicitly prohibited. Sexual intercourse should be genital to genital and in no other way. It should be between husband and wife and between no other persons. In any other way or between any other persons it is wrong and prohibited. A family is a mated pair raising its offspring in a home of its own. A family without a home, a husband, a wife, or a child is not complete. It is broken. A son or daughter by definition shares its parents' biogenetic substance. Exceptions to this may be provided for on legal grounds, by adoption, and fictions may be acceptable under special conditions. But insofar as it is possible, a son or daughter should be the biological offspring of both its parents.

But sexual intercourse also is, and stands for, love. The definitions of American culture state that love is spiritual and enduring and is not aimed at specific narrow material ends. Love is a relation between persons, not between things. It means unity, not difference. It means who you are, not how well you perform. It means trust, faith, affection, support, loyalty, help when it is needed, and the kind of help that is needed. Love means that one is never forsaken, betrayed, or abandoned. Love is freely and unselfishly given, or it is not really love in American culture.

The family, then, as a paradigm for how kinship relations are to be conducted and to what end, specifies that relations between members of the family are those of love. One can speak of the family as "the loved ones." Love can be translated freely as *enduring diffuse solidarity*. The end to which family relations are conducted is the well-being of the family as a whole and of each of its members.

Yet certain specific acts which are part of the cluster of symbols that define kinship and family also have the value of signs for other symbols of that defining cluster. Sexual intercourse between husband and wife is not only an act which specifically defines the conjugal relationship, but it is also an act which is a sign of love. Not only is adultery wrong because by definition sexual intercourse is the distinctive feature of the conjugal relationship, but it is also a sign that the love which is embodied in sexual intercourse is directed at someone other than the person who has a right to it. The act of adultery is thus more than simply a wrong. It is an act which is both wrong in itself and at the same time a sign that something more is wrong as well, that love is no longer where it should be. For adultery is treated as an act of disloyalty and betrayal in a way that can be understood only if the act is something much more than merely an event of sexual intercourse. It means that the spouse is not loved; it means that the love which should be exclusive to the married couple has been given to someone who has no right to it; it means that the very essence of the spiritual relationship between a man and wife has been treated as a mere form of gratification, animal, not human, in its meaning. In adultery, it is love which is at stake, as well as sexual intercourse.

Enduring, diffuse solidarity, or love, in its most general sense in American culture is doing what is good for or right for the other person, without regard for its effect on the doer. Indeed, its effect on the doer is good and beneficial by virtue of the good it does. What this may consist of as a specific act is not given in the symbol of love or of enduring, diffuse solidarity, but is instead located in all of the other context-defining symbols of American culture. The right thing to do for a middle-aged man may be the wrong thing for a child. What is good for an upper-class woman may be bad for a woman of lower class. What is kind to a farmer may be an offense to an artist.

One of the most important things about love, or enduring, diffuse solidarity, is the fact that such a wide variety of different kinds of specific acts can express or affirm it. In one context a kiss affirms love. In another context paying the rent does this; so does holding the job that earns the money to pay the rent. Holding a hand may express diffuse solidarity. Having the house clean and neat may be a sign of love. Cooking food may demonstrate love, and so can eating what has been cooked. For a man to tend a baby may express his love not only for the baby but for his wife, the baby's mother, as well. And for the wife to tend the baby may express her love not only for the baby but also for her husband, the baby's father. To tell the truth may be the essence of diffuse solidarity in one context, and to tell a lie may be its highest expression in another.

But by the very same token, the sign of love in the wrong context or the wrong way may be the sign that there is no love. Having the house so neat and clean that it cannot be lived in may not express solidarity at all, but only that the other person does not really belong in the house, that it is not his home. To work so hard to get the money to pay the rent that there is no time for anything except work may be the simplest way of saying that there is no love. This is hardly an act of solidarity, diffuse or otherwise.

In summary, then, the family in American kinship as a paradigm for how members of the family should conduct themselves is essentially a very simple one. A system of a small number of symbols defines and differentiates the members of the family. These same symbols also define and differentiate the kinds of relationships—that is, the codes for conduct—which members of the family should have with each other.

The members of the family are defined in terms of sexual intercourse as a reproductive act, stressing the sexual relationship between husband

and wife and the biological identity between parent and child, and between siblings. There are two opposite kinds of relations here. One is between opposites, husband and wife. Out of their union their child is created. The child is of the same biogenetic substance as its parents; this unity of material substance maintains the unity of parent and child and sibling when the child is first differentiated by its birth, and then when he continues to grow apart by growing up, marrying, and founding his own family. The fundamental contrast is between the unification of opposites—husband and wife in sexual intercourse—and the maintenance of the unity of those who are differentiating—child from parents and sibling from sibling.

The symbol of love bridges the two culturally distinguished domains, first, the domain of kinship as a relationship of substance, and second, the domain of kinship as a code for conduct, for the kind of interpersonal relationship between and among them.

Sexual intercourse is love and stands as a sign of love, and love stands for sexual intercourse and is a sign of it. The two different kinds of love, conjugal and cognatic, the one erotic, the other not, are nevertheless both symbols for unity, identity, oneness, togetherness, belonging. Love symbolizes loyalty, faith, support, help, and so forth.

However the members of the family are differentiated from one another, then, their relationship to each other should be identical. It should be one of love. Each should act toward the others with love as the guiding principle. Or, as it is said more accurately, with love in his heart.

As a kind of relationship, love can be translated as *enduring, diffuse solidarity. Solidarity* because the relationship is supportive, helpful, and cooperative; it rests on trust and the other can be trusted. *Diffuse* because it is not narrowly confined to a specific goal or a specific kind of behavior. Two athletes may cooperate and support each other for the duration of the game and for the purpose of winning the game, but be indifferent to each other otherwise. Two members of the family cannot be indifferent to one another, and since their cooperation does not have a specific goal or a specific limited time in mind, it is *enduring*.

The biological elements in the definition of kinship have the quality of symbols. That blood relatives share biogenetic substance is a symbol of unity, of oneness, and this is symbolically interchangeable with the symbol of love. The biologically stated symbols of unity are variously restated in American kinship; the child's being of the body of its mother; created jointly by the bodies of both mother and father; its taking nourishment from its mother's breast; the notion of the milk of human kindness and the ultimately unqualified unreserved safety and trust which the breast stands for; the child's taking after or looking like and acting like its parents and its parents' parents—all these are special applications of the general statement that biological unity is the symbol for all other kinds of unity including, most importantly, that of relationships of enduring diffuse solidarity.

Kinship in American culture, then, is a relationship of enduring diffuse solidarity. Yet this is not quite enough to distinguish it from all other kinds of relationships. Friends, in America, can be loyal, faithful, helpful, and everything which a relative can be. It is even said, facetiously, no doubt, that a boy's best friend is his mother, though it is also said that a man's best friend is his dog. However incompatible such statements seem to be, they are nevertheless of the same order and directly to the point.

Friendship and kinship in American culture are both relationships of diffuse solidarity. What distinguishes friends from relatives, as informants tell us so clearly, is that you are born with your relatives but you can pick your friends. If you can pick them, by the same token they can be dropped at will and without obligation. Of course, loyalty to a friend is vital and to let a friend down when he is in dire need is inexcusable. But it is also true, as one statement has it, that with such friends, who needs an enemy?

The contrast between friends and enemies is that where friends act out of love, enemies act out of hate. Where friends have one's best interests at heart, the others carefully select the worst interests to amplify.

Relatives are related by blood or by marriage; friends and enemies are found or chosen or are self-selected, but they are certainly not given to one at birth, as are relatives.

We have no difficulty distinguishing friends from relatives. In this regard, friends and enemies are alike in being chosen. In regard to how they should act, friends and relatives are alike in that they are both guided by the norms of diffuse solidarity.

Here, perhaps, is the key to the matter.

In the contrast between home and work, there is that interstitial area, that peculiar domain that combines the best parts of each, but is neither, called the vacation, a commercial undertaking which provides a home away from home. Friendship, like a vacation, provides the best parts of the two distinct domains and is of this same interstitial quality.

Where one is born with one's relatives, and one's diffuse solidarity is with them "for life," one can pick and choose one's friends at will and with certain clear purposes in mind. So it is said, of course, that as one rises in the social ladder, the character—the social character, that is—of one's friends changes to reflect that rise. Although one may choose a spouse, for one is certainly not born with one, there is nevertheless a fundamental difference between the two. A spouse is for better or worse, for the long run, and the quality of the loyalty (or love) is enduring and without qualification of time or place or context. To pick a spouse and shed a spouse for purely utilitarian purposes is not considered proper, though it certainly is done.

Where an employee is held to rigorous standards of performance within a specific domain of relevant action, a spouse is not, but instead is held to standards of diffuse solidarity. A spouse is either loyal or disloyal, faithful or unfaithful. There is no measure of efficiency in a spouse's fidelity. There is no measure of skilled accomplishment in a spouse's loyalty. One hopes for the best but takes what one gets.

But a friend is dropped if the friend fails to maintain desirable standards of loyalty, or solidarity, or fidelity. Performance in a friend is everything, for there is nothing else. A good friend is one who executes the tasks of loyalty with skill and courage and dispatch. A good friend is there in time of need, and does not bumble the job. And a good friend is dropped for failing to meet the proper standards of performance in the role of diffuse solidarity.

Friendship combines the advantages of freedom to evaluate performance and terminate the relationship with the requirements of diffuse solidarity, which do not specify exactly what a friend has to do. Friends are relatives who can be ditched if necessary, and relatives are friends who are with you through thick and thin whether you like it or not and whether they do their job properly or not. You can really count on your relatives.

It is this, of course, which makes sense of the phrase that a boy's best friend is his mother and a man's best friend is his dog. A mother will and sometimes can do things for a son which meet the highest performance standards of friendship. Her performance may be more than is merely required by the enduring relationship of mother and son. And a dog, just because you can demand the highest standards of loyalty, of diffuse solidarity, from him, is a kind of friend; it is not a hireling or a paid agent, because the diffuse solidarity occurs in a context where you can get rid of the dog if you want to. Here, of course, the contrast with one's own children is the clearest. One expects diffuse solidarity and loyalty from one's own children. But if they turn mean, they cannot be taken to the local humane society to be "put away." They are yours and you stay with them as they stay with you.

PART TWO

THE RELATIVE AS A PERSON

CHAPTER FOUR

A Relative Is a Person

The decision as to who is and who is not a relative is made by and about a *person*.

The person is a major unit of American culture, just as the family, the company, the city, and the country (the nation) are cultural units.

These units are different from other kinds in that they are defined by American culture as being able to do something or *to act*. It is an explicit legal "fiction" that the corporation is a person, capable of acting for good or for ill, and of being responsible for its actions. So, too, the country can act. It can go to war, spend money, have a foreign policy. Just as it can be said that a person does something, so, too, it can be said that a city or town or company or country *does* something.

The person, as a cultural unit capable of action, has a *primary identity*. This defines what kind of person he is; that is, it defines the relevant cultural domain in terms of which he acts. A person may be a father, a policeman, a judge, a priest, a pilot. The father is a person in a family. The policeman is a person in the police department, which is part of government. A judge is a member of the court, which is part of government and the law, while the priest is a member of a church, which is the domain of religion.

Different elements are blended together to make up the definition of the person, but such elements must make up a unit defined as doing something, playing a role in real life. The policeman is a man. He acts to maintain law and order. He must know the law to do his job, though the policeman is certainly not a lawyer, nor is the lawyer a policeman. He must know how to read and write and be able to issue a legal summons for infractions of the law where this is appropriate, though knowing how to read and write hardly makes a man a policeman. He must be able to defend himself against physical attack and use force where necessary to apprehend criminals, though just being physically strong and a good fighter does not make a man a policeman.

The different elements which are combined into the definition of the person—policeman, father, judge, or whatever—come from different systems of concepts and symbols, each from its own domain, which is defined apart from persons or other such qualifications. In American culture, maleness and femaleness have certain definitions, certain attributes, which are defined quite apart from any person, any situation, or any special restriction of context. Age, too, is defined in American culture apart from any particular situation or any particular person, though it plays a part in the definition of a variety of different kinds of persons. And so too, kinship forms its own self-contained, distinct set of concepts and symbols defined apart from person, place, or time.

In the last chapter I examined the culturally explicit meanings of the family, those which direct observation and informants readily provide. In those meanings, the family is a married couple with their children living together in a home of their own, or it is the married couple and their children without regard to where they are living, or it is a much wider unit which includes what is said to be all, or nearly all, of those persons who are counted as relatives.

In these senses the family can mean Mr. and Mrs. Jones and the three little Joneses, or it can mean the hundred or so persons who attend the annual Jones family picnic and reunion. And in this meaning too, but pointing from past to present instead of just to the present alone, is the usage which says that the Jones family is a very old family indeed, having been in this town since it was first settled, more than 150 years ago.

Those meanings are given in terms of persons, and the task of the last chapter was to take that set of meanings of the family and to refract out its various conceptual and symbolic components so that the kinship part could be isolated in its pure form, so to speak, in contrast to all of the other components out of which those person-based definitions are constructed.

For instance, informants say that a wife cooks and keeps house, and observation often confirms this. But does the wife do this because she is a *wife* or because she is a *woman?* The answer is clear from informants as well as observation; she cooks and keeps house because she is a *woman.* Women who are not wives cook and keep house; wives do not necessarily cook and keep house. Cooking and keeping house does not make a woman a wife. The distinctive feature which defines a wife is that she is the legitimate sexual partner of her husband. Similarly, a husband, some informants say, should go to work and earn a living to support his family. But does a husband go to work and earn a living because he is a *husband?* The answer from informants is that it is a man's job to work. But a man is not necessarily a husband, and a husband does not necessarily work. What makes a man a husband is not that he works or does not work, but that he is the legitimate sexual partner—the mate, it is sometimes called—of his wife. In the same way, informants are clear that it is proper for a father to have authority over his children. But again the question can be put: Does the father have authority because he is the father? The answer is that he does not. A father has authority because he is male and because he is older, not because he is a father. The authority of the father over his children wanes with their coming of age; therefore, their age has much to do with his degree and kind of authority. The distinctive feature of being a father or a husband has nothing to do with authority at all. A father is a genitor, and as our informant put it, a husband is a lover.

So we found that in American kinship the family is a paradigm for what each relative is and how they should behave toward each other. And this means, as I have shown, that the father is the genitor, the mother the genetrix, husband and wife in sexual relationship, son and daughter the offspring of that union, brother and sister the children of the married couple, and the relationship of all of these to each other one of love, either conjugal (husband and wife) or cognatic (the others), but in either case, love is a relationship of enduring, diffuse solidarity.

The family in *this* sense consists of the self-contained set of symbols differentiated out of the central symbol of sexual intercourse/love. It defines what a relative is in the abstract. It states what the relationship between relatives is by definition. It consists of a set of conceptual elements and their interrelationships.

This, in brief, is what American kinship consists of, and these, in turn, are elements which inform any particular person, insofar as he is a relative or undertakes a relationship of kinship.

But kinship, as a self-contained system of symbols and concepts defined and differentiated without reference to person, place, or time, is distinct, in American culture, from relatives as *persons* and the family as a *group of persons*. The two must not be confused or confounded, for they are quite different. *The relative as a person is quite different from the distinctive features which define the person as a relative.*

A person as a cultural unit is a composite, a compound of a variety of different elements from different symbolic subsystems or domains. The person has either male or female sex as defined by the sex-role system.

The person has age attributes as defined by the age-role system. The person has class characteristics as defined by the class system. The person may have occupational, religious, political, or a variety of other attributes, each defined by reference to its own self-contained set of symbols from its domain.

It is the construct of the person which articulates the various conceptual and symbolic domains of American culture and translates them into actable form; that is, into a set of normative standards, or guides for action, to which any concrete, actual person can orient this action.

In American culture the person is conceptualized as concrete as well as abstract, both as a set of normative standards *and* as a real, living individual who should try to behave in accordance with those norms. There is not only the person who is wife and mother in a family, as a culturally defined construct, but there is also a particular person to whom one can point and say, "*This* is my wife, John's mother." The family is conceived of as a concrete group of persons, but the family also has its concrete counterpart, as well as its abstract conceptualization. "This," one can say to a visitor, "is my family: this is my wife, Mary; this is my son, John; this is my daughter, Jane; and we all live together in this house, which is our home." But one can also speak about the family as a group of persons, consisting of the husband and wife and their children living together in a home of their own, without having any particular person in mind.

The family in this sense, as a group of persons, is the same order of cultural construct as the church as a body of worshippers, a baseball team as a group of players, a university as a community of scholars, or, in some other societies, a lineage as a corporate local descent group.

This brings me to the final point which must be made here about the relative as a person.

I have said that the person is a cultural construct so defined as to be able to act, to play a role in real life. The construct of the person is, in this sense, a normative guide for how such a person should behave or how such a person should act.

Love has two kinds of implications for how relatives should behave toward each other. The first is, of course, with reference to the very specific set of symbols in terms of which the kinship system as a whole is defined and differentiated, namely, sexual intercourse. Here the paradigm is quite explicit. There should be no sexual intercourse between blood relatives, for their love is cognatic, but there should be, as a sign of love, *and* as love itself, sexual intercourse between husband and wife, for their love is conjugal.

But the second set of implications which love has for how relatives should behave toward each other can only be summed up in the most general of all guides to action: enduring, diffuse solidarity.

Now it is possible, in real life, to engage in sexual intercourse or to avoid it. But it is difficult in real life to go about in a state of love, manifesting enduring, diffuse solidarity.

Love, in this meaning, must be expressed or represented by some specific act which is its sign, but is not "it." The acts which can represent enduring, diffuse solidarity are almost infinite in their variety, over and above the specific symbol by which it is defined—sexual intercourse. And so love can be expressed, in American culture, by working hard or by not working too hard; by helping with the dishes or by not helping with them; by helping with the baby or by letting the mother take care of it; by mowing the lawn or by not mowing it.

There is nothing inherent, nor is there anything specifically defined in American culture, about love which makes any particular sign necessarily one of love or not-love.

There is, then, a very loose, indeterminate connection between the general state of enduring, diffuse solidarity and the particular or specific signs which are taken to mark it. The signs thus necessarily take certain of their meanings from areas apart from and beyond the bounds of kinship or family, and being defined as good or bad, as beneficial or harmful, as desirable or undesirable with reference to their own domains or systems of symbols, their value within the context of the family is established. But that act, with that value from that domain, is but one element in the blend which is the definition of the relative as a person and which defines the proprieties of his behavior as a person.

In sum, the relative as a person is quite different from the distinctive features which define the person as a relative. Moreover, there are two different kinds of persons in American culture. There is the abstract person, which is a normative construct, and the concrete individual. The self-contained set of symbols of which American kinship is composed constitutes the distinctive features which define the person as a relative. But the person as a relative is made up of distinctive features other than just those of kinship. Features from the sex-role, age-role stratification and other systems are all included in the construction of the person as a relative. The distinctive feature of the way in which relatives should behave toward each other is specified by the symbol of love, which can be understood to mean diffuse, enduring solidarity. But love, or diffuse, enduring solidarity is the most flexible of symbols, for it can be expressed in a wide variety of different ways, differently for women than for men, for adult members of the family than for children in the family, and so on.

Finally, it should be made quite clear that I speak here of the person as a unit of American culture and as a cultural category, and not as an analytic construct.*

II.

It is not enough, however, to know that the relative as a person is a compound of elements from different systems of symbols, all from within American culture. One more thing must be known, and that is the rule according to which a relative is compounded (formed).

The rule is very simple. A person is a relative if he is related by blood or marriage and provided he is closely enough related (or is not too distant).

Like any rule, its application depends on the meaning of the terms in which it is cast. If the meaning of the terms "blood," "marriage," "distance," and "relative" (or "related") is clear, then the application of the rule should be clear. I have already described the meanings of these terms in American kinship, and it only remains to show how they operate in the "compounding" or formation of a relative both as a normative construct and as a decision about a concrete individual.

It is a fundamental premise of the American kinship system that blood is a substance and that this is quite distinct from the kind of relationship, the code for conduct, the pattern for behavior, the model for feelings and sentiments, or the formulation of rights and duties which persons who share that substance, blood, are supposed to have. This distinction is the same as that between relationship as substance and relationship as code for conduct, and this, in another form, is found in the classification of relatives in nature, relatives in law, and the "blood" relatives who are relatives in both law and nature.

Since these two elements are quite distinct, each can occur alone or

---

* There is a considerable body of literature on the person, individual, actor, self, and so on as a useful analytic tool in understanding social behavior. None of this is immediately relevant here since my objective is to describe the cultural categories and not to analyse how they actually work. Martin Silverman used the person as a cultural category in his thesis on Rambi. I know of only two others whose work is directly relevant to my usage here. One is Clifford Geertz' "Person, Time and Conduct in Bali: An Essay in Cultural Analysis," *Cultural Report Series No. 14* Southeast Asia Studies, Yale University, 1966. The other is the work of Louis Dumont, who treats the individual (or person) as a category of Western culture in general. See his "The Modern Conception of the Individual: Notes On Its Genesis," and "The Functional Equivalents of the Individual in Caste Society," both of which appear in Volume VIII of *Contributions to Indian Sociology*, Mouton, 1965. See also his important book *Homo Hierarchicus* (Paris: Gallimard, 1966).

they can occur in combination, as is evident from the classification of relatives.

And since the two elements are quite distinct and each can occur alone as well as in combination, a person can base his decision as to who to count and who not to count as a relative on either one or on the other of these elements, or on both if they are present. In addition, the normative construct of a relative or of a particular kind or category of relative can also be "compounded" of either one or the other element, or of both.

These elements of substance and code for conduct, however, are not of equal value and their different values alone and in combination, along with "distance," account for much of the variance in the system at the level of the person, both as decisions about concrete individuals and as normative constructs.

Substance has the highest value, code for conduct less value, but the two together (that is, the "blood" relatives) have the highest value of all.

This means that where either element occurs alone, relatives of greater "distance" will be counted as kin or as relatives if there is only a substantive element present than if there is only the relationship or code-for-conduct element.

Another way of putting this which will be found useful is that if a person plays a kinship role or undertakes a kinship relationship (as a code for conduct) lacking any substantive element, or vice versa, he may or may not be counted as a relative, but he is more likely to be counted as a relative if only substance is present than if code for conduct alone is present; with both elements present he is most likely to be counted as a relative.

There is a correlative set of meanings here which are particularly important. Any given kinship term—father, mother, uncle, aunt, cousin, etc.—can be used to mean either the substance element or the code-for-conduct element, or both together. It is not always possible, therefore, to infer from a given usage whether it is the substance, the code, or both which is being denoted in a particular instance. It goes without saying that these two elements hardly exhaust the meanings of kinship terms; they also may be used to mean things in addition to, or other than, these two meanings.

I will now cite the statements of two different informants which illustrate, in very abbreviated form, not only the separability of substance and code for conduct (or, as informants sometimes put it, of blood from relationship), but also the way in which this separability occurs and its role in the decision to "count" a person as a relative or not. (In both of the following, *I* stands for Informant, *A* for Anthropologist.)

I: You want like my son-in-law's parents? No, I never see or hear of them. They're not related to me.

A: Do you have to be close to someone to have them related to you?

I: Yes. You use the relationship. When it drifts away you are no more related. You see I went to one of my husband's cousin's bridal showers. It was for a first cousin's bride-to-be. You only meet all these people there. You meet them like at weddings or showers, or bar mitzvahs or funerals. For these things they call on you and I answer the roll call. [Shrugs her shoulders as if to say, "What could be more simple?"] You walk in and you meet them all and half of them are pregnant, so you say, "How nice that you are going to have a baby, congratulations on becoming a new mother," and they say, "But I got two at home already." So you see how it is.

A: So are these people related to you?

I: They are when you meet them like that, but when you leave them, they're not any more.

A: They are not related between weddings and funerals, but they are during them?

I: Yeah.

A: Have they ever been related to you except at things like weddings and funerals and bar mitzvahs?

I: Oh, sure, but they aren't now. You see this business of being related to someone has to do with sociability. There are social cousins.

A: Can you give me any kind of rule for the person who is related to you?

I: Well, they got to be sociable with you or they're not related.

A: All right, but some of the people you named are related to you by blood, right?

I: Yeah, you get them by accident. You can't do anything about them —and grandchildren are the bloodiest!

A: Then you have relatives by accident. Your father's sister had children, right?

I: Yeah.

A: So they are related to you by blood.

I: No, they're not related. They'd have to be social. They were at one time, they aren't now.

A: Do any of your female first cousins have husbands?

I: Yes.

A: Are they your cousins?

I: I never see them.

A: Are their children related to you?

I: No, because I never saw them.

A: Your father's sisters—were they married?

I: Yeah.

A: Were their husbands considered uncles?

I: No, I never saw them.

(2)

A: Now. Your mother's aunt you mentioned, XXXX. Do you know how to spell that?

I: Nope. . . . [I's wife then spells it correctly.]

A: Did she have a family?

I: Yes. I know her husband is dead, but she has some children.

A: Do you consider them related?

I: I would if I knew them. I can't even think of their names now. We were not close to aunt XXXX.

A: I see. You feel you have to know someone, or at least know their name, for you to think of them as a relative?

I: Yes. There has to be some personality there. Otherwise if you go back far you and I are related, and that's about as weak as you can get!

A: Your mother's aunt XXXX—do you know exactly how she is related?

I: I think she's my mother's mother's sister, but that's my idea! I know my mother is very solicitous of her when she's here. There's a family get-together . . . it's an occasion.

"Distance" is simply the statement of kinship in quantitative terms. That is, on the one hand it is a measure of the degree to which two persons share common biogenetic substance, and on the other hand it is a statement of the magnitude of the claim on diffuse, enduring solidarity. If diffuse, enduring solidarity obtains, distance is the statement of "just how much." A relationship which is "close" is one where the claim is high; one which is "distant" or "far away" is one where the claim is smaller. "How much" can mean both the magnitude and that magnitude which is expressed by differences of kind. One kind may be "too much" or "too little" for a given relative. Kind, thus, is one form of statement of magnitude within the context of distance as a measure of diffuse, enduring solidarity.

The different value attached to substance as against code for conduct holds in the measurement of distance too. Insofar as the persons concerned are blood relatives, the degree to which they share a common heredity is the first measure of distance which is applied to them; it is this measure which is modified by other aspects of distance and not the other way around. If, however, there is no substantive element, then distance depends entirely on the code-for-conduct or relationship element.

"Marriage" is the relationship between husband and wife, entered into voluntarily and maintained by mutual consent. A person is related to another person "by marriage" when that other person is his spouse. But "by marriage" is also the term for that class of relatives related in law as opposed to by blood, and it therefore stands for those who are related by that code for conduct as well as for the code for conduct itself quite apart from the persons. "Marriage" and "in law" thus overlap in parts of their meanings; where they do so they may be used interchangeably. The overlap or shared meaning consists in the relationship as a code for conduct; that is, diffuse, enduring solidarity undertaken voluntarily and maintained by mutual consent. A relationship of "marriage" or a relationship "in law" obtains when it is one of enduring, diffuse solidarity. This is stated in the marriage vows by the phrase ". . . until death do us part." A relationship of enduring, diffuse solidarity with sexual intercourse as the legitimate and proper form of its expression is that between husband and wife. This is the sense in which "marriage" differs from all other relations "in law."

This, then, is the rule according to which concrete persons name other concrete persons as their relatives or as non-relatives, and according to which normative constructs are formed for relatives as distinct from persons who are not relatives. For particular classes of relatives, normative constructs merely add the specific distinctive feature for that particular kind of relative, so that, for instance, the father and mother ,as relatives are distinguished by the fact that one is genitor, the other genetrix. To form the norm for a husband, the norm for a relative is taken and altered to exclude biological substance shared in some degree less than some specified proportion (the distance element), and the code for conduct is specified as "the legitimate sexual partner of the other spouse." Then, from the sex-role-differentiation system, the definition of male sex is added, which distinguishes the husband from the wife. Further specification of the normative construct can be drawn from other systems of symbols, so that the stratification system may add the specifications of middle-class status in certain ways, while the standards of urban southern residence may contribute symbols from that domain.

III.

If we turn now to some empirical generalizations drawn directly from the field materials, the operation of the rule in its various formulations can be seen clearly. The material has not been "translated" into a form consonant with the exposition of the previous section. Rather, it remains as first-order generalizations, the form most readily recognizable by an observer.

The materials in this section center on the decision to count concrete persons as relatives. In the next chapter, using material on in-laws and kinship terms, the focus will be on the person as a normative construct.

One of the first things that anyone who works with American genealogies notices is that the system is quite clear as long as one takes Ego as the point of reference and does not venture far from there. As one goes out from Ego—in any direction—things get more and more fuzzy. This boundary fuzziness, or fadeout, is seen in a number of different ways. Most fundamental, of course, is the fact that there is no formal, clear, categorical limit to the range of kinsmen. Or, to put it in another way, the decision as to whether a particular person is or is not to be counted as a relative is not given in any simple categorical sense. One cannot say that all second cousins are relatives, but all third cousins are not. An American can, if he wishes, count a third cousin as a kinsman while a second cousin is actually alive but unknown, or known to be alive but nevertheless not counted as a relative.

The fadeout is also seen in the increasing uncertainty over names, ages, occupations, and places of residence the farther out the relatives are from Ego.

There is one particularly interesting way in which boundary fuzziness is expressed; this is through the Famous Relative. During the course of the field work we not infrequently encountered the statement that So-and-So, a famous personage, was a relative. Sometimes the relationship was traceable, sometimes not. When it was traceable, it could clearly be seen that this was the only relative of such distance on the genealogy, whereas closer relatives were unknown and unheard of.[1]

Yet another observation that is part of this picture is what I have called the "Christmas-tree effect." American genealogies are often not more than three or four generations deep; they take the form of a squat

[1] Compare M. Young and H. Geertz, "Old Age in London and San Francisco: Some Families Compared," *British Journal of Sociology*, XII (1961), 124-41.

Christmas tree or pyramid. At the top, there is often the Ancestor, sometimes in the form of a couple, like the star on a Christmas tree. As generations get closer to Ego, each sib-set somehow gets larger, so that the
whole thing seems to stand on a very firm, broad base. But if one looks
closely below the base one can see the trunk of the Christmas tree; Ego's
line, his children and grandchildren, who continue to move away from
Ego generation by generation. The Ancestor may or may not have had
siblings, but if he did, they are either not mentioned or they are forgotten. Sib-sets of the Ancestor's children are larger, while the sib-sets
and the collateral lines of cousins give the zero generation a considerable
collateral spread of both cousins and siblings.

The squat Christmas tree consists in a network of blood relatives. This
consanguineal network is adorned with spouses, like the decorations on a
Christmas tree. But the adorning spouses only occasionally have siblings
or parents, and the occasional spouses' parents only rarely have siblings.

One can take a genealogy in a wholly nondirective way by simply asking for a list of relatives and then asking if there are any more. Or one
can take a very systematic genealogy using probes of the utmost spec-
ificity such as: "And has he any brothers? sisters? mother? father? sons?
daughters? wife? (or husband)." In the first instance, the tree is rather
skimpy. In the second, the tree is quite bushy and about one-third more
persons are usually added to the genealogy. However, the basic shape
remains very much the same, because informants don't remember if
great-grandfather had any brothers or sisters; if he had, who they married; and if they married, how many children they had. As far as great-
grandfather's wife is concerned, if she is remembered at all, informants
imagine that she must have had a father and mother, but they do not
know their names, or if she had any brothers or sisters, or what their
names might have been.

There are two important points to note about the Christmas-tree effect
in American genealogies. The first is that they are pyramids of greater
or lesser range, but they include far fewer kinsmen than the definition
of a relative as anyone related by blood or marriage would lead one to
expect.

The second point is that they are fundamentally consanguineal networks to which spouses are added. In-laws are not common; in fact, they
are notable by their absence. In genealogies, informants normally list
their own spouse and the spouses of their blood relatives, but they do
not often spontaneously list the parents or siblings of any of the spouses
they list, and often not even the parents and siblings of their own spouse.
There were a number of exceptions. In one extreme case, a man listed his
mother's sister's husband's brother and sisters and their husbands and

wives and children. These were the only brothers and sisters of the spouses of blood relatives that he listed spontaneously, although it turned out that he knew others and could easily name them. Asked if he considered these to be relatives, he affirmed that he did.

Closely related to this point is another of some relevance. Of the two theoretically possible ways of increasing the number of kinsmen actively engaged in a particular network, it is those who are related by marriage who constitute a major source of additional numbers rather than the wider spread which would be obtained by tracing back further and then out to more widely placed collateral lines. It is by the addition of the consanguineals of spouses rather than by the increase in the number of more distant collateral lines of consanguineal kinsmen that the size of networks tends to be augmented in America.

Nevertheless, when the situation warrants, the net can be spread very widely indeed, as the cousins clubs and family circles reported by Mitchell[2] show. When the net is spread this widely, there is again a choice among kinds of links, so some organizations require blood connection through a founding ancestor while others permit the addition of members *through* spouses as well as *to* spouses.

The decision as to who is a relative is made by and about a person. Sometimes the decision which a person makes about another person is common and usual, and informants agree that it is the "right" decision. But sometimes, although the decision "makes sense" to informants, some may regard it as eccentric or even as "wrong." Such decisions, right or wrong, are nevertheless illuminating because they reveal the crucial elements which are involved.

The dead are a case in point.

The only standardized question asked of informants in Chicago was the first question of the very first interview. This was, "List for me all the people whom you consider to be your relatives."

All informants would start listing people, but some of them would suddenly interrupt the recitation with the question, "Do you want the dead ones too?" Or they would say, "What about those who are dead?" Or, "That's all, except for the dead ones, of course. . . ." It sometimes took the form: ". . . and Uncle Jim—but he's dead. . . ." But with almost every informant there was always something special about the dead ones, some remark, some comment, and almost invariably, if the person being listed was dead, this fact was spontaneously stated. Further, there seemed to be a clear tendency for the dead to be omitted entirely in the very

---

[2] W. E. Mitchell, "Descent Groups Among the New York City Jews," *Jewish Journal of Sociology*, 3 (1961), 121-28.

early phases of the collection of the genealogy, and only to come to light during later enquiry, often in another connection.

Another example is in the categories used to describe the fuzzy, faded area containing distant relatives. One of these is the term "shirt-tail relations," another is "wakes-and-weddings relatives," and the third is "kissin' kin" or "kissin' cousins." Wakes-and-weddings relatives are easily defined —they are, quite expectably, relatives who are only seen at wakes and weddings. Usually there is no direct contact, or even indirect contact, and some informants describe them as "relatives of relatives." Informants sometimes associate the term with Catholics, since in their view wakes are primarily a Catholic practice. Shirt-tail relations are very much the same, except that instead of specifying where certain relatives are seen (wakes and weddings), these are described as being "brought in on somebody's shirt-tail"; that is, they are seen as related through intermediaries and their main significance is that they are relatives' relatives. The terms "kissin' kin" or "kissin' cousins" are said to be primarily southern, though many Chicago informants knew the term even when they did not use it themselves. Here the kiss is the sign that no matter how distant, such persons are nevertheless relatives and therefore are entitled to that sign of being relative, the kiss.[3]

Yet another example is one I have already mentioned, that of the Famous Relative. (See page 67.)

Two examples of the understandable, but perhaps eccentric decisions on who is counted as a relative are the following: One woman firmly asserted that her sister was not a relative because she had not seen her or spoken to her for some years now. I did not have great confidence in this informant, and in other ways she proved difficult to work with. Since this statement seemed in plain conflict with the fact that a blood relative always remains a blood relative, I at first dismissed her statement as absurd. I was wrong to do this, of course.

A young lady attending college raised the opposite problem; she affirmed, and could not be dissuaded from the position, that her roommate was a relative even though she claimed no connection of blood or marriage between them.

Why should the dead constitute a problem? In discussing the question of whether it is possible to terminate a blood relationship, some informants said that it is, in fact, possible to do. Some Jewish informants de-

---

[3] Some informants say that the term is also used in another, and obviously closely related sense. If a person is seen with a stranger in a compromising position—perhaps they are seen kissing—one may offer the explanation that the other is a kissin' cousin. That is, though he is not recognized as being a relative by the observer, the kiss is explained as being one of kinship and not to be otherwise interpreted.

scribed a modified mourning ceremony which could be performed, according to certain religious and ritual prescriptions, by a parent to terminate the relationship to a child. This ritual could be performed only by a parent, not by a child. After this ritual the child was as if dead, and did not exist for the parent. So, these informants said, it was really possible, after all, for there to be an ex-child just as there can be an ex-spouse. The fact that this ritual is very rarely performed makes no difference. For informants who were not Jewish, the same situation could obtain, but it had neither ritual nor religious setting. A parent might simply terminate his relationship to the child, and act as if the child were dead by never seeing it again, and never speaking of it or with it. In this case the initiative could be taken by the child—since there is no formal rite—and the child could leave home and never speak to the parent again, acting as if the parent were dead.

When a Jewish parent holds a mourning ceremony for a live child (or a dead child), what is terminated is the *relationship* between them, but the child, as a child, is not "taken back" or made never to have existed. The Jewish parent, so moved as to have to hold a mourning ceremony for a child, is the object of special sympathy and pity, for the greatest tragedy of all has befallen him—his child, who need not have died, must now be treated as dead! This parent has lost a child. But he *had* a child, and the child is "there" and remains there.

It is perhaps obvious now why informants listing relatives stop and give the dead a special place: "Do you want me to list the dead ones too?"—for death terminates a relationship but does not undo or erase what is and was a fact. A dead person remains person enough to be located on a genealogy; person enough to be counted as an ascendant or descendant; person enough to be remembered if there is some reason to do so. Marriage is ". . . until death do us part." The *person* was and is; the *relationship* is no longer. Hence the half-status which is implied by the question, "Do you want the dead ones too?" An anthropologist asking politely, "Well, what do you think? Do you count them as relatives?" would be answered variously, "Oh, yes, of course," or "Well, yes, I guess so. But it's been so long now . . . ," or "No, not really."

The lady who said that her sister was not a relative because she had not seen her for so long was making the same point. She no longer had a relationship with her sister, and in this sense the sister failed to meet one of the defining criteria of a relative. For this woman the most important criterion was exactly the same as in the case of the other young lady, who valued a relationship above all things and so bestowed a kinsman's status on her roommate, even though the roommate lacked any other qualifications.

The Famous Relative is important because he stands out clearly against a fading groundwork of disappearing kinsmen. The blood connection can be traced to him, or is presumed to obtain. But no relationship can be maintained. Since no relationship is maintained with relatives of even closer genealogical distance, they are largely or wholly forgotten. Their names are forgotten, the names of their spouses, where they may be living, what their occupations are. They are, simply, not remembered because there is no good reason to remember them. But the Famous Relative is remembered—not because he is a relative, but because his fame makes his being a relative of some small value.

Shirt-tail relations, wakes-and-weddings relatives, and kissin' kin are so far out that they are neither here nor there. If one says that anyone related by blood or marriage is a relative, then they are relatives. But if one says that a relative is someone with whom a relationship obtains, then it is hard to count them, since they are seen so rarely, and then mainly on formal, ceremonial, or special occasions, and since the next occasion may or may not ever arrive.

There is, in sum, a tendency to forget distant collaterals and distant ascendants, but the boundary in either the past or the present is fuzzy and there are interstitial areas which are so faded at any given moment as to be barely visible. The distant ascendants are dead and no relationship obtains with them. Without a relationship, there can be no reason to retain them . . . unless, of course, they are famous, in which case they may be remembered though their descendants along collateral lines, lacking fame, will not be known. The distant collaterals "are too far away." They become shirt-tail relations, wakes-and-weddings relatives, and kissin' kin if they are known at all, or they may be one of the chief constituents of the large summer family picnic or reunion.

Americans say explicitly that relatives are persons related by blood or marriage. Yet when it comes to naming and describing concrete persons, the crucial question is whether or not a relationship obtains.

What, then, determines whether a relationship will exist or not? Why is there a relationship with one person but not with another on a given genealogy?

The reason Americans give is that one is "close" and the other is "too far away."

Distance, then, is said to be the deciding factor, given that a relationship of blood or marriage can be traced between Ego and some other person.

But what is distance?

Distance means three things in American kinship. One meaning is simple physical distance; that is, it means living in the same house, or the number of miles between houses, or the hours it takes to travel from one place to another. So one hears it said: "We never see them. They're too far away." "Too far away?" "Yes, it takes almost an hour to get there."

A second meaning of distance is a complex composite of what might be called socio-emotional distance. This in turn can mean anything from a mystical feeling of identity or difference, a feeling of emotional warmth and understanding—or the lack of it—to the fact that certain important prestige symbols are either similar (hence close) or different (hence distant). Thus it may be said, "We never see them. They're pretty far off. That part of town has gone way downhill in the last few years and we don't have much in common with them any more." Another informant put it this way: ". . . no one has had much to do with them either. It's a matter of the kind of life and education—hardly any of the people in her or Harry's family have been to college and that sort of thing."

The third meaning of distance can be called genealogical distance. This may be roughly measured by how many intervening categories of relatives there are, or how many generations back one must go before a common ancestor is found. It may be said, for instance, "They're pretty distant relatives. My great-grandfather's brother had a son, and he had a son—that's a pretty distant relationship, isn't it?"

These three different meanings of distance need not all apply in the same way or at the same time. A person who is genealogically close may be physically distant and neutral on the socio-emotional dimension. Or a person may be close socioemotionally and physically but distant genealogically.

If Ego is the point of reference, and we pose the direct question of whether, in real life, this person or that one is or is not a relative, then mother, father, brother, sister, son, and daughter, along with husband and wife, are all genealogically close relatives and are socio-emotionally close even when they may be physically distant. Uncle, aunt, nephew, niece, grandfather, grandmother, grandson, granddaughter, and cousin are also genealogically close relatives and are counted as relatives if they are alive, even if the relationship is so thin as to be barely perceptible.

But if we go out from Ego to his second or third cousins, many possibilities present themselves. Ego may say that he counts these persons as relatives simply because they are related by blood. Or he may say with equal propriety that they are too distant, so distant in fact that he does not even know how to count them. He may then ask, "What is a second cousin, anyway? And what does 'removed' mean?" Or he may affirm that anyone past first cousin is no relative of his since he does not count past first cousins.[4] Even if he claims them as relatives on the score of being related by blood, he still may not maintain interpersonal ties with them and therefore he may say that he does not "really count them as relatives." Or, unwilling to go so far as *not* to count them as relatives, and so perhaps hurt people's feelings, he may assign them to that limbo called wakes-and-weddings relatives, shirt-tail relations, or kissin' kin.

By one definition there is no option: those related by blood or marriage are relatives. But in fact, the decision as to who is a relative is made on grounds that are by no means purely matters of kinship. The number of miles between houses or the number of hours it takes to go from one place to another are not in themselves matters of kinship. Neither do they stand for kinship in the sense that physical distance might be used to express genealogical distance. Physical distance *could* stand for genealogical distance, but it does not in American culture. It stands for socioemotional distance. It is not polite for people to say that others are beneath them socially, so they say that they live far away, or they are stamped with the rank of the neighborhood they live in. By the same token, it is not always easy to explain that one's relatives are socially superior and so one may tactfully say that it's a terrible trip across town, all that distance, just to see them. But this is not genealogical distance.

One of our informants explained that she knew that her grandfather's brother had three sons. Two of them were farmers in Nebraska and she did not know their names, if they were married or not, or if they had any children. But the third son, she said, became a lawyer and went to Washington, D. C., where he married and had two boys and a girl. The girl, she said, was about her own age. The two boys were named Robert and John, the girl named Mary. Yes, she does consider them her relatives. They are related by blood, aren't they? she asked. Why, then, did she know all about one brother but not about the other two? She was unable to answer that question.

Another informant put it even more simply, saying:

I frankly prefer not to be related to them. He is a river rat and she is a hillbilly, and they have five kids to prove it. Not that I'm saying one has to be successful and well off to be considered a relative, but goodness. . . .

---

[4] There are three ways of counting cousins. The first is not to count them. The second combines degrees of collateral distance with generation removal, so that my father's father's brother's son is my first cousin once removed. The third adds degrees of collateral distance and generational removal together, so that my father's father's brother's son is my second cousin and the word "removed" is not used. I did not find any ways of counting cousins other than these three.

In sum, the fuzzy boundary, the Famous Relative, the ambiguous notion of distance, and so on are all phenomena of American kinship which derive in part from the fact that at one level the relative is a person and the person of the relative is compounded of elements from a variety of different domains, only one of which is kinship. Hence whether a particular person is counted as a relative or not depends on how the general rule—a person is a relative if he is related by blood or by marriage—is applied. Because the decision as to who is and who is not a relative is made by and about a person, and because the rule governing who is and who is not a relative is so precisely ambiguous, the application of the rule leads to just such empirical regularities as I have here reviewed—a very fuzzy boundary to genealogies; what seem to be logical inconsistencies, such as the marvelous manipulation of the different meanings of words like "relationship" and "distance"; and that peculiar ambiguity which marks the dead—those relatives without relationships.

CHAPTER FIVE

In-laws and Kinship Terms

In the last chapter I tried to show that in American culture the relative has two distinct yet articulated meanings. First, there are the distinctive features which define the person as a relative. Second, the relative as a person is constructed of more than just the distinctive features drawn from the symbol system of kinship, and includes elements from the age-role system, the sex-role system, the stratification system, and so forth.

But the relative as a person has, in turn, two distinct yet articulated meanings. On the one hand, the relative as a person is a concrete construct in that it refers to the person as a living human being, a real individual. On the other hand, the relative as a person is a normative construct, a construct consisting of normative guides and standards in terms of which behavior should proceed. In the last chapter I showed how the rule for constructing a relative works when it operates at the level of decisions about concrete individuals. That is, I showed how it worked to include certain concrete individuals and exclude others and how in its various formulations, Ego has choices which he can make and which are essentially at his option, about which particular people to count as relatives.

In this chapter I turn to the description of how the rule works at the level of the relative as a normative construct. Here, for example, it is not so much the question of whether Uncle Bill is, or is not, counted by informant John Jones as a relative. Instead it is the question of the normative standard which John Jones and other Americans use as a guide in reaching decisions about Uncle Bill and all of the other persons who may be considered relatives. It is, therefore, the question: What is an uncle? Can a mother's sister's husband be an uncle and if so, what kind, and if not, why not?

I have confined the discussion to relatives in law for two reasons. The first is that it will be far more useful to the reader to have one category of relatives carefully analysed in some depth and with some care than to have a few facile examples taken from here and there.

The second reason for selecting relatives in law for this particular exposition is that this category presents so many different yet fundamental problems.

I will once again proceed, therefore, by reporting first-order empirical generalizations from material collected in the field. It is in this form that any student of American kinship first encounters it and it presents itself as problematic precisely because it does not make immediate and self-evident sense. Apparent contradictions, ambiguity, and inconsistency mark this material.

Sections I and II of this chapter present these first-order empirical materials. Sections III through VII constitute not only an analysis of those materials, but include the introduction where it is relevant of further empirical materials. Sections III through VII should not, therefore, be regarded as simply analytic, for crucial steps in the analysis are only possible in the light of the empirical materials which must, therefore, be presented at that time.

The contrast between relatives by blood and relatives by marriage is very sharply put in American kinship. Although "relative" is used to include both relatives by blood and by marriage it is also used in a more limited, specific, or marked sense to mean relatives by blood alone, as opposed to relatives in law. When asked, Americans may properly say that their husband or wife is not a relative, but an in-law or someone related by marriage.

To begin with, the matter seems clear enough. There are two distinct classes of relatives by marriage; each is related in a different way. The first, of course, is Ego's own husband or wife. These relatives are distinguished by basic kinship terms. The second class consists of the mother, father, brother, and sister of Ego's own spouse, along with the spouse of Ego's brother, sister, son, or daughter. All of these take derivative terms and the in-law modifier. (See Table II.)

Some informants say that, strictly speaking, one's in-laws are one's spouse's closest blood relatives; that is, one's mother-in-law, father-in-law, brother-in-law, and sister-in-law. These informants say that although I am an in-law to my son's wife or my daughter's husband, they are not precisely in-laws to me, though they are, of course, daughter-in-law and son-in-law.

But "in-law" is also used for anyone related in any way by any marriage. Thus, although a man's wife's brother is his brother-in-law, his wife's sister's husband is not, and his wife's brother's wife is not his sister-in-law. Yet informants say that they think of a wife's sister's husband or a wife's brother's wife as being related "by marriage" and as being "an in-law of some kind." And the phrase "by marriage" can be combined with any of the basic kinship terms, so that one may hear of a "nephew by marriage" or a "cousin by marriage," etc.

There is still another use of "in-laws"; that is as a kind of collective designation for anyone in any way connected through one's own spouse. People may have what they describe as "in-law troubles" and so may designate their "in-laws" as "outlaws," or they may find themselves obliged to spend Christmas or Thanksgiving with their "in-laws." An inventory of who is included in that collective designation might include persons with whom only the vaguest if any relationship can be traced. Yet the designation makes a certain amount of sense since Ego's own link to them is through his spouse and so is "in law," whatever the precise nature of their linkage may be to Ego's own spouse.

Finally, "in-law" or "by marriage" is also used by some informants for anyone who is related to a spouse of one of Ego's own blood relatives. Thus, a man's father's sister's husband's mother, father, brother, sister, along with the brother's wife, and sister's husband can all be described as related "by marriage" or "in law."

There are at least the following distinguishable classes which can be and sometimes are designated as "in-laws" and "related by marriage," by some informants. (See Table II.) First, there is Ego's own spouse, for whom there is a basic kinship term, husband and wife. Second, there are the closest blood relatives of Ego's own spouse and the spouse of Ego's closest blood relatives; namely, mother-in-law, father-in-law, brother-in-law, sister-in-law, son-in-law, and daughter-in-law. These all have derivative kin terms. Third, there are those who are relatives of one's own spouse, however they may be related to one's spouse, who are not otherwise noted above. These would be, for instance, a spouse's mother's brother and his wife. Except for spouse's sibling's son and daughter, "nephew" and "niece," informants do not agree on the proper kinship terms, if any, for these. Fourth, there are those who are the spouses of any of the remainder of Ego's blood relatives; that is, all those except daughter's husband and son's wife. This would include, for instance, a cousin's wife or a niece's husband. Of these, informants are agreed only on aunt's husband and uncle's wife, kinship terms for whom are "uncle"

Table II.
"In Laws" or Relatives by Marriage

Class	Examples	Kin Terms
1. Own spouse	Hu, Wi	Husband, Wife
2.		
(a) Own spouse's closest blood relatives	SpMo, SpFa, SpBr, SpSi	Mother-in-law, Father-in-law, Brother-in-law, etc.
(b) Spouse of Ego's own closest blood relatives	SoSp, DaSp, BrSp, SiSp, FaWi, MoHu	Daughter-in-law, son-in-law, sister-in-law, etc. Step-mother, Step-father
3.		
(a) Own spouse's other relatives (except those in 2.a)	SpMoBr, SpMoBrWi, SpFaMo, SpFaBrSo, SpFaBrSoWi, etc.	?
(b) Spouse's sibling's children	SpSiSo, SpSiDa, SpBrSo, SpBrDa	Nephew, Niece
4.		
(a) Spouses of any of Ego's own blood relatives (except 2.b and 4.b)	Consanguine's spouse. FaBrSoWi, FaSiDaHu, SoSoWi, SoDaHu, etc.	?
(b) Uncle's and aunt's spouse	MoBrWi, FaBrWi, MoSiHu, FaSiHu	Uncle, Aunt
5.		
(a) & (b) Relatives of the spouses of Ego's blood relatives	MoBrWiBr & Si, MoSiHuBr & Si, FaFaBrWiSi & Br	?

and "aunt" respectively. These are the reciprocals of nephew and niece in the third class above. The fifth class consists of the relatives of the spouses of Ego's blood relatives: a son's or daughter's spouse's mother and father, for instance, or a mother's brother's wife's brother and sister and their husband and wife. Informants offer no specific kinship terms for these, or when they do, do not agree on the correct or proper terms.

The ambiguities of the phrases "in-laws" and "by marriage" begin to appear when we consider the fact that different ways of tracing connections "by marriage" are possible and that the phrase itself does not seem to require that one way be chosen over another. Moreover, kinship terms are applied to certain persons in ways which seem to suggest that they are examples of the meaning of that phrase and that they therefore can be taken as guides to its proper use.

Difficulties start from the fact that a son's wife and daughter's husband are "daughter-in-law" and "son-in-law," but uncle's wife and aunt's husband do not take the in-law modifier at all. They are, informants say, "aunt" and "uncle," and they are not distinguished from blood relatives by those kinship terms. "Aunt" can be father's sister, father's brother's wife, mother's sister, or mother's brother's wife. "Uncle" can be father's brother, father's sister's husband, mother's brother, or mother's sister's husband.

If a son's wife is a "daughter-in-law," and an uncle's wife is an "aunt," what then is a cousin's wife? By the "daughter-in-law" example she might be a "cousin-in-law," but she is not called this very often. By the aunt example she might be a "cousin," and some people do call them "cousin," but many people say that there is no kinship term for a cousin's spouse. Of those who say there is no proper kinship term for a cousin's spouse, some say that these are not relatives, while others say that they are relatives by marriage but without special names.

What, then, happens to "nephew" and "niece"? On the one hand, since "nephew" and "niece" are the reciprocals of "uncle" and "aunt," these terms include both a sibling's child and a spouse's sibling's child, thereby classing blood relatives with those by marriage just as in the case of "uncle" and "aunt." On the other hand, as in the case of "cousin," it is often said that the spouse of a nephew or a niece does not have a kinship term. Sometimes one hears the phrase "nephew (niece) by marriage," for some or all of these. Here it is even more problematic, since the nephew or niece may be (a) a sibling's child or (b) a spouse's sibling's child. The spouse of a sibling's child is like the spouse of a cousin; some informants say that they are "nephew" and "niece," and some say that there is no term for them. The spouse of a spouse's sibling's child is considered to be an in-law by some informants but not by others and of those who consider them relatives by marriage, only some hold nephew and niece to be the proper kinship term.

Death, divorce, and remarriage all raise special problems which further complicate matters. Here again the problem of the uncle or aunt married to a blood relative can be a source of some uncertainty.

It seems reasonably clear to many informants that the husband of an aunt or the wife of an uncle are uncle and aunt, respectively, only as long as they are married. This follows from the fact that they are uncle and aunt just because they are the husband of an aunt or the wife or an uncle. When they are no longer related by marriage, that is, when the marriage is over because of death or divorce, then they are no longer related and therefore are no longer uncle or aunt.

Nevertheless, some informants say that if a person has developed a special relationship with an aunt's husband or an uncle's wife, or likes them very much, then even if the marriage breaks up, it does not mean that they are no longer uncle and aunt. They remain uncle and aunt because of Ego's relationship directly to them. So, these informants say, if the aunt remarries, her next husband is not their uncle because they already have an uncle! The same situation would hold true if the uncle died and the aunt remarried. For some informants an uncle is an uncle when a special relationship obtains directly with him, and so too an aunt.[1]

In discussing this problem with children, a different view occasionally emerges. A few children say that if an aunt's husband or an uncle's wife dies or is divorced, they nevertheless remain uncle and aunt, respectively, and their successors do not become uncle and aunt. The reason given is that even though the uncle and aunt were related first by marriage, they remain uncle and aunt because they are the child's cousins' mother and father. As these children put it, "He is my uncle anyway because he is my cousin's father." Here, it might seem, uncle and aunt become blood relatives. Because they are blood relatives, neither divorce nor remarriage alters their position.

A second problem which is raised by death or divorce is the problem of the step-relatives. The problem consists in the fact that although some Americans assert, many other Americans deny that these are relatives "by marriage" in the same way as father-in-law, mother-in-law, etc., are.

Where death or divorce leaves a person with children, and he remarries, then the new spouse is a step-parent to those children. In just the same way, if one of my parents is no longer married to the other because of death or divorce, and my remaining parent remarries, then the new

---

[1] See W. H. Goodenough, "Yankee Kinship Terminology: A Problem in Componential Analysis," in "Formal Semantic Analysis," ed. E. A. Hammel, *American Anthropologist*, 67:5, Part 2 (1965), 267. "A PaSi's or PaPaDa's second Hu is less assuredly *my uncle* than the first Hu if Ego has already established a relationship with the first Hu as *my uncle*," and he says the same thing for "my aunt." It is interesting that Goodenough did nothing with this very crucial piece of data. He neither resolved the question of what "less assuredly" means nor attempted to raise the important question of the significance of the phrase "a relationship." I noted this point in my critique of his paper, D. M. Schneider, "American Kin Terms and Terms for Kinsmen: A Critique of Goodenough's Componential Analysis of Yankee Kinship Terminology," in "Formal Semantic Analysis," ed. E. A. Hammel, *American Anthropologist*, 67:5, Part 2 (1965), footnote 4, p. 308.

spouse of my parent becomes my step-parent, and his children my step-siblings. But are they all my "relatives by marriage"?

Some Americans affirm that a mother-in-law and a step-mother have very little in common. One is a spouse's mother, the other is one's own mother, and these are very different.

Some informants say that an uncle's wife is an aunt and that she is a relative by marriage. Some informants say that an uncle's wife is an aunt, but that she is not really a relative at all, just an uncle's wife. Some informants say that an uncle's wife is an aunt and that she is a relative for so long as she is married to the uncle, but if she is divorced or if the uncle dies, she is no longer a relative. These informants add that it is polite to continue to call her "aunt Sally" just as before, if the uncle dies. But if the uncle and aunt were divorced it depends. If the uncle died, she may continue to see the family just as she used to. Some children say that she is their aunt no matter whether she is divorced or the uncle is dead, because she is their cousin's mother. And some say she is their aunt if they like her, but not if they don't.

This situation is substantially the same for the aunt's husband, for the grandfather's second wife who is not the parent's mother (or his third wife, for that matter), for the grandmother's second husband who is not the parent's father (or her third husband). It is also approximately the same, but with certain significant differences, for the spouse's sibling's child, nephew, and niece, the reciprocal of the uncle's wife (aunt) and aunt's husband (uncle). That is, for my father's sister's husband, I am his wife's brother's child.

There is one important asymmetrical bias to all of this. The informant who is firm about counting his uncle's wife as an aunt and as a relative is much less firm about his spouse's sibling's child. He does not address that child as "nephew" or "niece," and he may say that he does not feel as close to his spouse's sibling's child as he feels to his uncle's wife or his aunt's husband. When informants are asked to compare their spouse's sibling's child with their uncle's or aunt's spouse there is much less assurance about the spouse's sibling's child being a niece or nephew than there is about the uncle's or aunt's spouse being an aunt or uncle, or even being a relative. Further, informants often resort to a rather odd form of logic, which reads: "If my aunt's husband is my uncle, then I am his wife's sibling's child, and if he is my uncle then I must be his nephew." The opposite avenue of argument, that *because* I am his nephew he must be my uncle, is not only seldom offered spontaneously, but when informants are asked to try it they say that the whole formula sounds very odd or awkward to them, though they may not be able to put into words just what is wrong with it.

This asymmetry is especially marked when the spouse's sibling's child happens to be the child of the sibling of an ex-spouse. After the divorce, whatever the child may say, the informant may be quite firm about the fact that his ex-wife's or ex-husband's sibling's child is not really a nephew or niece at all. But, indeed, here again it is important to note that informants volunteer that this often depends on the relationship with the child, the ex-spouse, the sibling of the ex-spouse, the parents of the ex-spouse, how long they were married, how well they got on with their in-laws, and so forth.

A second asymmetry which should be noted is in the way in which the kinship terms are applied. Though I address my aunt's husband as "uncle Bill," he does not call me "nephew." For him *not* to use a kinship term is correct and proper usage; for me to fail to use a kinship term may be considered to be disrespectful. In the same way, in the context of identification, one may say of an aunt's husband, "He is my uncle," and leave it at that. Children tend to identify uncles and aunts quickly and easily in just that way and without qualification unless specifically pressed with such questions as: "And just how is he related to you?" But informants do not hesitate to identify a person as "my nephew by marriage" or "niece by marriage." "She is my wife's niece" or "he is my husband's nephew" are common usages.

II.

But this is only to raise the question of the meaning and uses of kinship terms in American kinship. Why should children tend to identify their aunt's husband and uncle's wife as "my uncle" and "my aunt," while adults reciprocate by saying, "She is my wife's niece" or "he is my husband's nephew"?

Any discussion of kinship terms with informants tends to move immediately into the frame of *Who Is Called What and By Whom*. No matter how one asks the questions, they all seem to lead right back to the firm ground of specifying who calls whom what. Yes, informants say, I have heard the word "pop" used. But then they go on to talk about how much difference it makes who calls whom "pop."

Who, then, is called what and by whom in American kinship?

The first point which must be made is that there is a wide variety of *alternate* terms and usages applicable to any particular kind of person as a relative. To put it another way, there are far more kinship terms and terms for kinsmen than there are kinds of kinsmen, or categories of kinsmen.

Mother may be called "mother," "mom," "ma," "mummy," "mama," "old woman," or by her first name, nickname, a diminutive, or a variety of other designations, including unique or idiosyncratic appellations, sometimes related to baby-talk. Father may be called "father," "pop," "pa," "dad," "daddy," "old man," "boss," or by his first name, nickname, a diminutive, or a variety of less commonly used designations, including unique or idiosyncratic appellations, sometimes related to baby-talk. Uncles may be addressed or referred to as uncle-plus-first-name, first name alone, or uncle alone. And so, too, aunts. Grandparents may be called "grandma," "grandpa," "gramma," "grapa," "nana"; last names may be added to distinguish "Gramma Jones" from "Gramma Smith." Cousins are addressed by their first name, nickname, a diminutive, or other personal form of designation, or as cousin-plus-first-name ("Cousin Jill"). Son may be called "son," "sonny," "kid," "kiddy," "boy," or by his first name, nickname, a diminutive, or other forms of personal designation. And daughter may be called "girl," "sister," "daughter," by her first name, nickname, a diminutive, or sister-plus-first-name ("Sister Jane"), as well as idiosyncratic and personal forms. "Kid" as a form for child does not distinguish son from daughter. Brother may be "brother," brother-plus-first-name, first name alone, nickname, diminutives, or personal forms. Sister may be "sister," sister-plus-first-name, first name alone, nickname, diminutives, or personal forms.

The use of personal pronouns and variations in specifying to whom the relationship is further increases the number of alternatives. Mother, for instance, may be "my mother" or just "mother." One may refer to a third person by his relationship to the speaker ("my mother"), to the person spoken to ("your mother"), or, as in teknonymy, to someone else ("Tom's mother"), as well as by some attribute or quality ("the great mother").

Some informants call their spouse's parents by parental terms; that is, spouse's mother is "mother," "ma," "mom," etc., while father is "father," "pa," "pop," "dad," etc. Some use a parental-plus-name form such as Mother Smith (Father Smith), Mother Jane (Father Jim), or Ma Perkins (Pa Perkins). First-naming is also used here, but informants are often quick to state that first-naming is not always the first name used. If they met as strangers there is a tendency toward Mr. and Mrs.-plus-last-name forms, and only later when the spouse's parent permits or invites it is the first-name form used. Informants are also quick to note the prevalence of no-naming [2] here. One informant in his mid-fifties, married for more than twenty years, claimed that he had never addressed his wife's mother by any form whatever! If it was absolutely necessary to get her attention

___

[2] This is the zero form of address. It may sometimes be articulated as a throat clearing or "uh hum" sort of noise. Erving Goffman first suggested the term "no-naming" to me some years ago.

he made coughing or throat-clearing noises, to which she had learned to respond.

Where a parent-in-law is first-named with his permission or on his invitation, a sibling-in-law may or may not stand on such ceremony. Forms for siblings-in-law are the same as those available to siblings.

Usage varies with who is being spoken *to* and who is being spoken *about*. One informant refers to his mother as "mother" when speaking to his father, as "ma" or "mom" when speaking to his brother, and as "my mother" when speaking to his uncle (his mother's brother) or with a stranger. Another informant, who says he usually calls his mother-in-law "mom" when speaking with his wife about her, studiously avoids calling her anything when his own mother is present (no-naming). Another informant calls his father's brother "Uncle Bill" when speaking with his father, "Bill" when speaking to his father's brother directly, provided no one else is present, and "my uncle" when telling stories about his exploits to some friend who does not know him.

Some informants say that they rarely if ever confine themselves to a single term for any given kinsman. Some of these informants say that they use a "principal" form and "alternate" forms, but other informants do not find it easy to say which is a principal, and which an alternate form.

Where all informants are willing to list "dad" and "daddy" as forms which they could use with any other father term, some informants say that "father" and "pop" are incompatible. That is, if Ego uses "father" he is unlikely, and unwilling, to use "pop" or "pa." Conversely, if Ego uses "pop" or "pa," he is unlikely to use "father" with any regularity. On the other hand, "dad" is compatible with any and all of the alternate terms.

Informants who use "father" explained that they would seldom if ever use "pop" or "pa" because it was entirely too familiar and somehow did not imply the measure of respect that was required. Those who use "pop" or "pa" take the same position, but from the other side. They would seldom use "father," they say, because it implies authority and respect in greater measure than either they or their father deemed appropriate, and more formality and impersonal distance than was desirable. This is not to say that "pop" or "pa" or "dad" imply any lack of respect or any absence of authority. Quite the contrary. It is just that these qualities are not the salient ones in those terms.

Informants do not divide the terms for mother into such incompatible categories, but the sex of the speaker seems important here. Informants said that "ma" and "mom" were less likely to be used by daughters than by sons, and that "mother" was more acceptable to daughters than to sons.

The formal term "father" is not the precise analog of the formal term "mother." "Father" has formality and authority and respect implications which "mother" does not share. For instance, some male informants reported that when they argued with their fathers they would avoid any form of address (no-naming again), and one informant reported that if, during an argument with his father, he used the term, he would feel forced to abandon the argument: "You shouldn't argue with your father!" By avoiding the use of the term, he was not forced to face the transgression that was implied.

On the other hand, male informants who reported that they would avoid any form of address while arguing with their father readily stated that an argument with their mother included such exclamations as, "Oh, mother!" and, "But, mom, how can you say such a thing?" That is, there was no such inhibition on the use of the term "mother" as there was on the use of the term "father."

If in one respect informants say that they use "father" terms differently from "mother" terms, in another respect they use them in the same way. As small children it is appropriate for both males and females to use "daddy," "mommy," or "mummy"—that is, informal or diminutive terms. But men from the North say that as they grow up they drop "daddy," feeling it to be childish or effeminate, while women may keep "daddy" or shift to "father."

Informants sometimes report the use of first names alone for both uncles and aunts. In working over particular genealogies with informants, it is obvious that some informants do not apply any particular term consistently for all aunts or for all uncles. That is, one informant called his mother's elder brother "Uncle Jim" and his mother's younger brother "Bill." Another reported that he called his mother's sister "Aunt Jane" and his mother's sister's husband "John."

When is the "aunt" or "uncle" term plus first name proper, as against first name alone?

Some informants say that they prefer to use first name alone for aunts on the mother's side rather than on the father's side and prefer to use the first name alone for males rather than for females.

Some informants say that they dropped "aunt" and "uncle" terms and used first names alone after they started going to college or after they felt grown-up enough. Some informants reported that where there was strong affect, either positive or negative, the "uncle" term would be dropped in favor of the first name alone. For instance, an informant with three uncles called one "John," one "Uncle Bill," and the other "Jim." He explained this by saying that the first person was a dirty so-and-so and that he would not dignify him by calling him "uncle." Asked why he did not call Jim "Uncle Jim," he explained, "Jim is a wonderful guy! He and I have always been the best friends!" And Uncle Bill? Uncle Bill was neutral, "a nice guy."

If the alternate terms for uncles and aunts consist of "uncle" or "aunt" alone, first name plus "uncle" or "aunt," and first name alone, one might say that there were only three alternate forms, and that three is not a very large number.

But there can be no such complaint about the terms for husband and wife. Here the elaboration of alternate terms goes much further than it does anywhere else in the American kinship system.

Terms for husband and wife fall into three rough categories: kinship terms, variations on one's given name (first name, nickname, diminutives, etc.), and a group that might be given special dignity and formality by being labeled "terms of endearment." Kinship terms are made up of two subcategories: first, terms used to indicate the order of kin, i.e., terms of identification that explain who he or she is, such as "my wife," "my husband," "Mrs. X," or "Mr. X"; second, parent terms, i.e., "mother," "mom," or "my old woman," for the wife, "father," "dad," or "my old man" for the husband. Terms of endearment fall into a series of classes: saccharine terms (honey, sugar, sweet, cookie, etc.), affection terms (love, beloved, lover, etc.), animal and vegetable terms (kitten, bear-cat, pumpkin, cabbage, etc.), and a large and varied collection of miscellaneous and idiosyncratic terms, some of them nonsense syllables (baby, pookums, etc.). We are all familiar with at least some of these terms. There is probably a greater variety of terms for wife than there is for husband.

Two other sets of alternate terms should be noted. The first is the grandparent, parent, spouse, sibling, child, and grandchild set. Here father and mother are "parent," husband and wife are "spouse," brother and sister are "sibling," and son and daughter are "child." This set treats the sex of the relative as without significance, but specifies generational discrepancies. In the set containing the ancestor, ancestress, and descendant, the sex of the relative is distinguished in the ascending generations but ignored in the descending generations, and the particular generation is ignored here as it is specified in the first of these two sets. The treatment of sex in this set is very much like the treatment of sex in the triad which is offered as the definition of the family; namely, mother, father, and child, or husband and wife and their children.

A particularly interesting set of usages is that in which a man uses "mother," "mom," "my old woman," or other parental terms for both his wife and his mother, and a woman uses "father," "dad," "my old man," or other parental terms for both her husband and father.

One context in which this occurs is when an adult speaks to his child about the child's other parent, and uses the child's term for that parent. A man will say to his son, "There is mother," or he may say, "Go to mother," "Give this to mother," or "Ask mother." A woman, of course, says the same things to her child, using the "father" terms for her husband.

Americans sometimes say that in dealing with children, particularly young children, they use the term the child would use; they add that this helps the child to learn. So, although I may be the child's mother or father, I would say to the child, "There is (your) father (or mother)."

This point may have some merit, but its two parts should be kept separate. There is a time in a child's life when all grown-ups are "mother" or "father"; this time is followed by a time when all grown-ups are "mother" and "father," but not necessarily their own. I encountered a child of about four, struggling with a knotted shoelace, who appealed to me: "Somebody's daddy! Please fix my shoelace." On another occasion I was told by a child to "Go ask your mother if you can come out and play with us," by which I understood him to mean that I should tell my wife; I knew that she was not my mother even if he did not. Such usages by children are not uncommon. They seem to be related to the fact that adults do use the child's terms for other adults, saying that they do this in order to help the child learn the proper usages.

In many cases of this sort, however, the children are not involved as children, or they are not involved at all. If I speak to my cousin about his mother I may say "your mother" or "Aunt Sally." When I say "your mother," I can do so whether he is a small child or a grown man. Surely a grown man does not need to learn that the lady is his mother, or what kinship term he should use for her.

The same is true for one's own child. One may say to one's own child, very small or fully grown, "Give this to mother." When I speak to my very small child or to my fully adult one about "grandfather" or "grandmother" rather than about "my father" or "my mother," I make a special point which is not in itself connected with my child's age. A woman who addresses her husband's mother as "grandma" may do this long after her child has grown up. But I can also speak to a child of any age about "my mother" and "my father," speaking of these persons in terms of their relationships to me and not to him. The manipulation of possessive pronouns also does not have much to do with the age of a child or even whether children are present. To say, "Give this to mother," is not the same as to say, "Give this to your mother" or "Give this to my mother." Under certain circumstances, when a man says to a child, "Give this to mother," it is not a matter of "your mother" so much as it is "*the* mother" in the family.

There is one final point which must be made in this connection, and that is about reciprocals. When a man addresses his wife by some "mother" term, she does not call him "son" except to make that point. And when a woman calls her husband "dad" or talks about him as "my old man," he does not reciprocate with "daughter" terms. The reciprocal of "mother" is "father" when the speakers are husband and wife, though of course it does not have to be. If a man calls his mother "mother," the reciprocal may well be a "son" term like his first name, though of course it does not have to be.

The pedagogic point is simply inadequate as an explanation, and so too is the "rule" that one uses the child's term for the adult. The fact of the matter is that we observed many cases where husbands who call their wives by "mother" terms, and wives who call their husbands by "father" terms, do not have any children, never have had any children, and have no prospect of ever having any children! They are using parental terms for each other in a way which cannot have anything to do with actual children, since there are no actual children involved.

III.

The uncertainties, inconsistencies, and ambiguities which seem to characterize the relatives by marriage and kinship terms are not in the system itself. Neither are they in the minds of the natives who act within its jurisdiction. Instead, they are in the mind of the observer who does not understand the cultural categories, how they are defined and differentiated, and how they articulate into a meaningful whole.

Just what is problematic about in-laws or relatives by marriage and kinship terms?

The problematic materials consist of the variance at many points and the apparently inexplicable absence of variance at others. The variance consists, for example, of the fact that uncle's wife and aunt's husband, some informants say, (a) are relatives; (b) are kinds of relatives called "aunt" and "uncle" respectively, along with parents' siblings; (c) these are the proper kinship terms for them; and (d) are members of the class of relatives called "relatives by marriage" or "in-law." But some informants deny either one or more of the items (a) through (d) above. Another example of variance that seems problematic is the cousin's spouse. Some informants say that a cousin's husband or wife is a relative, that "cousin" is the proper kinship term for such a relative, and that such relatives are members of the category "relative by marriage" or "in-law." Other informants say that a cousin's husband or wife is a cousin's husband or wife and not a relative at all, and that there is no kinship term for such a person. Yet other informants say that a cousin's husband or wife is a relative by marriage or an in-law, but that no special kinship term is proper to such a relative.

It is important to note, however, that the differences among informants —the variance in these data—are treated by informants as legitimate alternate or variant norms and not as deviant or illegitimate. They may say, for instance, that it would be wrong for them to count a cousin's husband as a "cousin," but they know that some people do, and that it is perfectly proper for them to do so. Another example is the fact that three modes of address for uncles and aunts are prevalent, each is regarded as perfectly proper, and the grounds on which one or another form is rejected by any particular speaker are considered to be matters of free personal choice, or matters connected with "our kind of people."

This kind of variance is in sharp contrast with the situation in regard to the distinctive features which define the person as a relative, which were presented in the first part of this book. If the total response—that is, all of the interviews and data collected from a given informant over a period of six to twenty-four months—of different informants is compared on such questions as, "What kin relationship, if any, is your genitor to you?" and "What kin relationship, if any, is your uncle's wife (or aunt's husband) to you?" there is not only a very high degree of agreement on responses to the first question, but variant responses or variant instances are treated as wrong, improper, and illegitimate, as errors of fact or judgment. The situation is just the reverse with the total responses to the second question, and variant responses are treated as legitimate alternatives.

But one further and most important fact must be emphasized. If informants are asked the second question, namely, "What kin relationship, if any, is your uncle's wife (or aunt's husband) to you?" they are almost unanimous in their *immediate* response. They almost always answer, "She is my aunt" or "He is my uncle." If a survey were taken of a random sample of Americans I have no doubt that an overwhelming majority of respondents would answer that question in just that way, and if the inquiry stopped there, that is all that would be learned.

The variance in the data only emerges after a variety of different questions have been framed and offered, after a variety of different observations have been elicited and discussed, and after the field worker has a substantial body of knowledge about the informant from his genealogy, his history, his experiences, and his interaction with members of his whole family.

One problem, then, is to account for the presence of alternate norms at this level and the absence of alternate norms at the level of the distinctive features themselves.

A second problem is to define and account for the kinds of alternate norms. What do the different definitions of uncle's wife and aunt's husband mean? What do they imply not only about the total system, but about the system at the level of the relative as a person?

A simple, and perhaps useful way to put these problems is to ask why there appear to be so many logical contradictions. Why should there be three or even four different names for a given kind of relative? Why should the father be "father," "pop," "dad," "my old man," etc., when surely the word "father" would seem sufficient for most purposes. Are these merely synonyms, different words with precisely the same meaning? Why should some people say that when an aunt divorces her husband or dies, he is no longer an uncle, while others say that he may or may not remain an uncle, depending on his relationship to Ego or the family? Why is there disagreement on such a simple matter as this? Is there no rule? Are these not logically contradictory alternatives? What is the rule, or what are the rules?

To answer such questions it is necessary to go back once again to the first principles of American kinship. It is a fundamental premise of the American kinship system that blood is a substance and that this is quite distinct from the kind of relationship or code for conduct which persons who share that substance, blood, are supposed to have. It is precisely on this distinction between relationship as *substance* and relationship as *code for conduct* that the classification of relatives in nature, relatives in law, and those who are related both in nature and in law, the blood relatives, rests.

Once again it is necessary to go to the next step; these two elements, substance and code for conduct, are quite distinct. Each can occur alone or they can occur in combination. Hence any particular person can base his decision as to who to count as a relative on either of these elements, or on both if they are present.

Substance or blood in its biogenetic sense is a state of affairs, a fact of life that nothing can change. Either it is there or it is not, and if it is there it cannot be altered or terminated. It is *involuntary*, then, in two senses: a person cannot choose to enter or not to enter into that state, and if he is in that state he has no control over it and cannot alter or terminate it.

The code-for-conduct or relationship element is quite the opposite. It is *voluntary* in the sense that it must be voluntarily undertaken—a person chooses to enter or not to enter into such a relationship—and the person has some control both over the particular form it takes and over whether or not it is to be terminated. The word "consent" is often associated with this element, and is most closely associated with one particular form of it, marriage.

This, then, is the situation of the divorced or widowed spouse of an aunt or uncle. As informants said so clearly,[3] "It all depends on the relationship." First, it depends on the relationship because it cannot depend on anything like substance—there is no substance on which to base a relationship. Second, if the relationship, the code for conduct, the pattern for behavior, is such that the family wants to maintain a relationship, then it does so and the relationship continues. But if by mutual consent they would heartily like to see the last of each other, then they have ample grounds for doing so. It is the substantive base, the common biogenetic substance that marks the obligatory condition, the condition that is binding and that cannot be terminated. A relationship that lacks such a substantive base lacks the binding permanency which substance entails.

But this is true for the spouse of an aunt or uncle regardless of whether they are divorced or not, and regardless of whether the aunt or uncle is dead or not; they are relatives, if they are relatives, only because theirs is a *relationship* of kinship, that is, only because they invoke that code for conduct which is one of kinship. It is not because there is some substantive basis which entails a relationship of kinship. Precisely because there is no substantive basis for it, theirs is a voluntary and optional relationship of kinship, one which depends on mutual consent. Voluntarily undertaken, it can be voluntarily broken. These are relatives because they *choose* to follow that code for conduct rather than some other code, not because they are *bound* to follow it.

The same is true for the whole area of relatives by marriage or relatives in law, including the major member of that category, the husband or wife. These are relatives only insofar as a code for conduct is invoked for them which is one of kinship. Their identity as persons who are relatives depends on this element alone. Because by normative definition it is optative and voluntary, different informants are free to act differently according to its very flexible rules, and are free to give very different answers to the simple question, "Do you consider him to be a relative?"

This can be put once again but in somewhat different terms by saying

---

[3] And as Goodenough's informant told him so plainly. See footnote 1, page 81.

that the word "relative" means three different things in American kinship. First, it means a person who is identified by another person as having some relationship of substance, as sharing biogenetic material. Such a person would be a relative in nature, and for convenience we might label him a "relative [1]." Second, it means a person who is identified by another as having some relationship in that he follows a code for conduct which is one of kinship. This would be a relationship of enduring, diffuse solidarity, but the forms in which this was expressed and precisely how firm and deep and abiding it was would depend on a variety of factors. Such a person would be a relative in law, and for convenience could be labeled a "relative [2]." Third, a relative is a person who is identified by another person as having some relationship both in nature and in law and so is called a blood relative. Since $1 + 2 = 3$, it is entirely appropriate to label him a "relative [3]."

When an American identifies another person as a relative he does not draw a sharp distinction between these three different kinds of relatives or these three different meanings of that word. Hence it is not always easy to tell just what is meant when an informant says "Oh, yes. My aunt's husband is a relative all right. He is a relative by marriage. One of my in-laws, I suppose. I call him 'uncle' you know!"

An aunt's husband and an uncle's wife, then, are relatives insofar as they voluntarily enter into and maintain the role of kinsmen, that is, insofar as they are relatives by mutual consent. It is just as legitimate and just as proper to affirm that such persons *are* relatives as it is to affirm that such persons *are not* relatives, since these are two alternate norms, each of which can be followed by different persons at the same time or by the same person at different times. That is, it is at the option of the persons themselves whether they will or will not maintain a relationship (as code for conduct) of kinship. Aunt's husband and uncle's wife can be taken as examples which stand for the whole category of relatives in law or relatives by marriage in this respect.

But if all this is true, how can it be true of the step- and the foster relatives, for if these are indeed relatives in law the very first question which must be answered is the question of consent. One may well and reasonably ask if a child really has much choice about whether he will voluntarily undertake and maintain a relationship of kinship with a step- or foster mother or a step- or foster father. For if anyone picks his stepmother it is his father who does so by picking a new wife, and if anyone picks his step-father it is his mother who does so when she picks a new husband, and if anyone chooses a foster family for a child it is most likely some court or social agency supervised by a court which has jurisdiction over the child. The child himself hardly makes the choice.

According to the definition of a child by American culture, a child has not yet reached what is called "the age of consent," and therefore his consent is given for him and on his behalf by someone who is or who stands for his parent. This holds until the child is competent to give it himself. And indeed, when he reaches the age of consent he may very well voluntarily terminate that relationship despite the many different pressures to maintain it. In the case of an adult whose mother or father remarries, the matter of consent is much more clearly evident for here the adult may easily and simply enter into or decline to enter into a relationship of kinship with his parent's new spouse.

One final point should be made here. I have spoken primarily with regard to specific kinds of relatives—aunt's husband, uncle's wife, step-mother, foster father, and so on. But in each instance the example can be taken for the whole category. Yet it is important to note explicitly one further point, since it may not be clear from a consideration of specific examples alone. This is that the *category* of relatives by marriage or in law in American kinship is *not* equal to or defined by the sum of its members, for the formal cultural definition of the category stipulates who *may* be included but not who *must* be included. Alternate norms govern which kind of member will be included by which kind of Ego at any given time. This follows from the fact that the category definition stipulates that the relationship is a matter of consent, that is, that it is voluntarily undertaken and voluntarily maintained.

It is this fact, then, which accounts for much, though by no means all, of the apparent ambiguity and contradictions which the first two sections of this chapter described (pp. 76 - 89). It is this fact which accounts for some informants saying that a cousin's spouse is a relative by marriage while other informants say that a cousin's spouse is a cousin's spouse and not a relative at all. It is this fact which accounts for some informants saying that when their aunt's husband got divorced he ceased from that moment (if not actually before!) to be their uncle, while other informants say that even if he is divorced he is still their uncle because he has established the relationship of uncle-nephew or -niece with them, a relationship not affected by the divorce. It is this fact which accounts for some informants saying that a spouse's uncle is their uncle, while other informants say that a spouse's uncle is a spouse's uncle and that he is not even an in-law to them! And it is this fact which accounts for the informant who says that while his Aunt Jane's husband is his uncle, his Aunt Alice's husband is a bum and no uncle to him! These are all equally legitimate alternate forms since they follow from the category definition which stipulates that a relative by marriage or in law is one with whom a relationship of kinship is undertaken by mutual consent and maintained by mutual consent, and that where consent is lacking there is no relationship in law.

IV.

The next problem which must be dealt with is the question of the phrases "by marriage" and "in law." Are these two phrases simply synonymous? It is not immediately self-evident why certain relatives are explicitly named by kinship terms which include the phrase or modifier "-in-law" ("mother-in-law," "father-in-law," etc.) while others who seem to fall in the same general category are not (cousin's spouse, nephew or niece's spouse, sibling's spouse's sibling, grandfather's second or third wife who is not parent's real mother, etc.). Neither is it self-evident why the whole category is called relatives "by marriage," since some of these are not related by marriage in any simple, self-evident way (the foster relatives for example). And even when some rationale can be presented showing that they are indeed related by marriage (as can for the step-relatives, for example) many informants are acutely uncomfortable with this and deny its validity even when they are stumped by its logic. Some informants try to explain "by marriage" to mean "by the marriage of any of my blood relatives," and thus to account for the uncle's wife and the aunt's husband as aunt and uncle respectively. But they are then hard-pressed to explain why they do not count their cousin's spouse as cousin —although other informants do—and the spouse of their nephew and niece as niece and nephew—although some other informants do. "By marriage" therefore is not a simple abbreviation for "by the marriage of any blood relative," although this is a tempting explanatory step for many informants to take.

To understand "by marriage" and "in law" as the names for this category we must go back once again to the first principles of American kinship. The American kinship system, as a system of symbols, is a special development from the major division of the universe into two parts, that of nature and that of law. Law, in the sense of an order which is created, invented, imposed, is thus opposed to nature, which is "given." Yet the regular processes of nature are regarded as conforming to "the laws of nature," and therefore law in its widest sense seems to mean order, regularity, and obedience to rules.

Although law is the category of widest scope, it is within the order of law at its widest that the particular opposition of nature and law occurs, formulated as an opposition between the two sources of order— the one which is "given" and the other which is "made." In the domain of kinship, then, law is that order which has been made for and imposed upon mankind and man's nature. Law at this level of contrast is thus specifically restricted to custom, tradition, the mores, and the ways of man as against any other way.

The fundamental symbol out of which the system of symbols of the American kinship system is differentiated is, as I have said, that of coitus. In the whole universe, which is divided into an order of nature and an order of law, it is the symbol of coitus which relates the kinship system to the universal system. The two parts of the symbol of coitus which are differentiated are, first, that of the substantive outcome—the child which shares the biogenetic material of its parents—and, second, the relationship (conduct) of the two parents to each other. The word for this latter aspect is "marriage"; it stands for the unity of the husband and wife, their unity in a sexual relationship, and a unity which is opposed to the unity of the parent and child.

Marriage, then, stands as *the* relationship in law which is specifically restricted to mean a sexual relationship, while all other relationships in law are not so restricted in their meaning.

Yet marriage and law stand in another relationship to each other. Law is the very broadest of terms, covering any kind of order in any domain of the world. But, even in its restricted sense as the order of law as against the order of nature, meaning the regularity imposed by human reason, this order of law far transcends the domain of kinship. That order of human reason which is within the domain of kinship is only one part of the whole order of law. To speak about a relationship in law, therefore, does not specify which suborder or which specific domain is intended.

Hence the term "marriage" is the exemplar of those relations in law *within* the domain of kinship. It is the very essence of the relationship in law of all of the different kinds of relationships in law within the domain of kinship. It is the example of a relationship in law within kinship *par excellence*. That is, although it is only one special and restricted kind of relationship in law, it is nevertheless its clearest and most vivid expression. It is in this sense that the formula: "a relative is a person related by blood or by marriage" is to be understood. Marriage is specified in the formula as if to say: not *any* relationship of *any* domain which is the relationship in law, but that order of relationship which is in law and also in the realm of kinship, as exemplified by the particular relationship of marriage.[4]

Marriage is thus a term which serves to stipulate the specific domain within the larger order of law.

The normative construct of the relative "by marriage" or "in law" as a

---

[4] J. H. Greenberg, *Language Universals* (The Hague: Mouton & Co., 1966), p. 28.

person, therefore, has the stipulation that, lacking a natural or substantive component, it consists of a particular code for conduct alone. As such, it is voluntary in that it is up to each party to enter into it, maintain it, or opt out of it. It is thus not obligatory in the same way as the blood relationship is obligatory, although it has its own canons of obligation which are essentially those of diffuse, enduring solidarity. Such a relationship thus depends, as informants put it, "on the relationship." It is called a relationship "by marriage" not because each of the two parties to it is married to each other, for they often are not, but because "by marriage" is the term for that specific kind of relationship which is, within the domain of kinship, the relationship "in law" *par excellence;* therefore, this is marked as a kinship relationship and not just any relationship which is orderly and lawful.

V.

Let us return once more to Table II. I presented this table as a simple way of summarizing some of the apparent contradictions and inconsistencies which first strike the observer when he reviews the field materials on the category of relatives in law. It is thus an artificial first-order fabrication which is quite inaccurate. For instance, the figure is incomplete and does not list all of those relatives who may be considered relatives in law. Only step-mother and step-father are listed among the many kinds of step-relatives who may be relatives in law. So too there are no foster relatives listed when foster relatives may well be relatives in law or relatives by marriage. The table is, therefore, quite incomplete even as a list of possible relatives in law.

But Table II has still one more purpose to serve before it is discarded completely, for we have not yet considered the last column on it called "kin terms."

In the kin terms column of Table II there are some basic terms ("husband," "wife," "uncle," etc.), some derivative terms ("mother-in-law," "step-mother," etc.), and some question marks.

I placed question marks in the kin term column of Table II when informants seemed to disagree on just what the proper kin terms should be. Where informants did not seem to be in any basic disagreement I inserted the term which they generally agreed on. Thus, for example, informants were generally if not universally agreed on the proper term for a spouse's mother, which they gave as "mother-in-law," and that term appears in the kin term column. But informants were not agreed on the kinship term for a cousin's spouse. Some said that a cousin's spouse is a cousin and should be called "cousin." But some said that a cousin's spouse is a cousin's spouse and nothing else and that they should not be called "cousin" since they are not cousins or even relatives at all. But other informants said that although a cousin's spouse is a relative by marriage, there is no proper kinship term for them and they are most appropriately called by their first name or whatever may be polite under the circumstances.

We can now see that each of these informants is correct, each in his own way. A cousin's spouse may or may not be considered a relative, for these are alternate forms. If he is considered a relative then he can only be a relative in law of course. If he is a relative in law, then a kinship term may or may not be considered to be properly used. This, too, depends on an alternate set of norms which regulate the definition of the relative as a person. One set of alternate norms specifies that a relative by marriage may be designated by the same kinship term as is used for his spouse (taking the sex of the relative into account where necessary). Thus if a mother's brother is "uncle," his wife may be termed "aunt" according to this set of norms; if a mother's brother's son is termed "cousin," his wife may be termed "cousin"; if a sibling's child is either "nephew" or "niece," the spouse of one of these may be termed "niece" or "nephew." But the other set of norms says that it is not necessary or even proper to apply a kinship term to relatives by marriage. Under this norm a cousin's spouse who is counted as a relative by marriage may still quite properly *not* be termed "cousin" by informants who follow this norm. And for some, but by no means all, of these latter informants, it is possible to append the suffix "by marriage" or "in law" to any kinship term, so that the constructions, for example, "cousin-in-law" or "cousin by marriage," "aunt-in-law" or "aunt by marriage" are held to be proper kinship terms.

One other set of alternates within the category of relative in law should be specifically mentioned. These are the step- and the foster relatives. For some informants there can be only step-mother, step-father, step-brother, step-sister, step-son, and step-daughter, and correspondingly these are the only derivative kinship terms which can be constructed from the modifier step- which these informants regard as proper. The same can be said for foster. For such informants a "step-aunt" or a "foster aunt" may be understandable constructs, but they are not proper kinship terms, nor would these informants regard their use as proper for them.

But for other informants the situation is quite different. For these informants any relative of a foster or a step-relative is a relative of their own. For these informants it is possible to have a step-grandmother or a foster grandfather, a step-uncle or a foster uncle, a step-cousin or a foster cousin, etc., simply because these are relatives of the key figures, the step- or foster relative through whom they are related. Correspondingly, and this point is important, such relatives take derivative kinship terms constructed from the modifiers step- and foster, so that the step-uncle, for instance, is given the proper kinship term "step-uncle," and the cousin of a foster mother may properly be given the kinship term "foster cousin," or the nephew of a step-mother may be properly a "step-nephew." [5]

VI.

The discussion of the preceding section has almost unconsciously followed a course which hides rather than reveals a very fundamental point. I have presented the discussion in this form: "A person may or may not be considered a relative in law; if he is considered a relative in law, then he may or may not be designated by a particular kinship term." This formulation suppresses the possibility that even though it is correct and proper to designate a person by a kinship term, that person may *not* be counted as a relative of any kind whatever. To put this in a somewhat different way, does it follow that an uncle's wife or an aunt's husband are counted as relatives *because* it is proper to call them "aunt" and "uncle" respectively? Are kinship terms necessarily terms for kinsmen in American culture?

Let us turn to kinship terms once more. American kinship terms are used as verbs and adjectives as well as nouns, and these ways of using them may be independent of each other even when they occur in the same utterance. I have heard a boy complain that his father "mothers him," and Americans who read the title to Edith Clark's book, *My Mother Who Fathered Me,* do not often mistake it for a monograph on parthenogenesis.

This is no more than to say that the fundamental distinction between relationship as substance and relationship as code for conduct in the American kinship system is such that any given kinship term can mean either the substance element alone, the code for conduct or role element alone, or it can mean both at once.

[5] W. H. Goodenough, 1965, *op. cit.*, gives an account in which the modifiers "step-," "-in-law," and "foster" are confined to the basic terms "father," "mother," "brother," "sister," "son," and "daughter." It is significant that Goodenough, at the outset of his text though not in its title of course, explains that he is dealing with the kinship terminology of only one person, which he knows is not shared in all respects by all North Americans or all native speakers of English. As I have already indicated, this pattern is indeed one of the legitimate alternate patterns of terminological forms in American kinship, but there are others which I have reported above.

Further, the kinship term may be used in such ways that either the substance meaning, the conduct meaning, or both may be implied at once, and the listener need not be told by the term itself which of these three meanings is indicated by any particular usage. Or, on the other hand, specific modifications may be made which do tell the listener which of the three meanings is intended or which is excluded.

And since kinship terms are applied to persons, one more combination occurs. Kinship terms may be applied to persons who are not kinsmen or relatives. When this occurs, the kinship term marks the role or code for conduct element. Sometimes, when this happens, the term is specifically modified so as to make this quite clear to the listener. But sometimes there is no such modification, nor is there any rule which requires any. It is therefore not possible to infer from the use of the kinship term alone that persons to whom they are applied are necessarily considered to be relatives.

Consider the following examples of these points. If a woman is a stepmother, mother-in-law, or foster mother she is clearly not the child's genetrix and thus not related to him by substance, though she does play one or another variant of the maternal role. But this is equally true for the den mother of a cub scout troop, the house mother of a school dormitory, and the mother superior of a convent. Note first that in each of these cases the way in which the term "mother" is modified defines the kind of person who plays that role, and each modification shows that the term "mother" means the role or conduct, and not the substance element. Note second that persons who are not kinsmen can be assigned kinship roles. Thus the person to whom the kinship term is applied may or may not be defined as a relative. This follows from the fact that a person is the object which takes a kinship term; the kinship term is not the object itself. And note third that the set of derivative terms is by no means exhausted by the "step-," "-in-law," and "foster" modifiers but must be considered to include "den," "house," and "superior," so that "step-mother," "mother-in-law," "foster mother," "den mother," "mother superior," etc. are all members of the same set.

But if a woman is both genetrix and plays a maternal role she is the child's "mother," and so too if she is not the genetrix but plays the maternal role after having legally adopted the child. Here there is no modification which specifies that one or the other element, or both, are implied. This is also true for the term "father." "Father" can be used for genitor and for priest; the first is a kinsman, the second is not. "Uncle" and "aunt" can be used for a parent's sibling or for a parent's friend; the first are kinsmen, the second are not. "Sister" can be used for a female sibling and for a female of slightly lower status; the first is a kinsman, the second is not. "Brother" can be used for a male sibling and for a male fellow lodge or church member; the first is a kinsman, the second is not. "Son" can be used for one's own male child and for any younger male; the first is a kinsman, the second is not. "Daughter" can be used for one's own female child or for any younger female; the first is a kinsman, the second is not.

The use of parental terms by a husband and wife for each other, both where children are relevant and where they are not, is a particularly good example of the fact that kinship terms can be used to invoke a particular role, because this is one of their meanings, and the terms can be used with reference to this meaning alone. A man who says to his own small child, "Give this to mother," does so to invoke the role of mother, defining that woman's identity as a person as that of a mother. The same man saying to the same small child "I won't have my wife treated that way young man," now invokes his own obligations to his wife and defines her identity as a person as his wife rather than as the mother in the family.

If kinship terms are not necessarily terms for kinsmen, what, then is a kinship term and how can a kinship term be distinguished from any other kind of term? The distinctive feature of kinship terms in American culture, as against any other kind, is that kinship terms have as one of their many meanings the biogenetic relationship or the code for the conduct of kinship (that is, diffuse enduring solidarity) or both. Other terms do not contain these meanings as their defining or distinctive features. For instance, friendship terms can be compared with kinship terms and distinguished from them by the fact that friendship terms exclude biogenetic relationship as a defining feature, and by the fact that the diffuse solidarity which is a feature of friendship terms is not *necessarily enduring* as a part of the distinctive features of its definition. Instead, its solidarity is contingent. This follows from the fact that the code for conduct of kinship is defined in terms of the symbol of biogenetic unity which is defined as enduring, and this biogenetic symbol is absent from friendship, as it is defined in American culture.

In sum, the fact that the uncle's wife and the aunt's husband are called "aunt" and "uncle" only means that some kind of a kinship role is invoked for them. They may or may not be regarded as relatives, for what they are called and whether they are counted as relatives are not the same questions. By the very same token, then, it is possible in American kinship to regard a person as a relative yet not find a kinship term associated with him. This is the case for some informants in regard to the spouse of a cousin who is not called "cousin," the spouse's sibling's child's spouse for whom the term "nephew" or "niece" is only occasionally invoked, and so on. Such persons would all be normatively constructed out of those elements which go to make up the general class of relatives by marriage or in law, while the other elements of their construction as a person would be defined by how old or how young they were, their sex, class items, and so on.

VII.

This still does not tell us all that we need to know in order to understand relatives by marriage or in laws or the uncle's wife or aunt's husband in particular. There is a very special kind of unanimity to informants' responses which has yet to be explained. Informants almost always say that uncle's wife and aunt's husband *should* be called by "aunt" and "uncle" terms, or that they themselves do so or have done so, or that they were instructed to do so by their parents, or that it is only after the nephew or niece has grown up—if then—that first-naming might be acceptable. This is in marked contrast to terms for cousin's spouse, the spouse of a nephew or niece, or the spouse of a spouse's sibling's child. In these latter situations informants often simply say that there are no terms for such relatives, or that they call them "cousin" or "nephew" or "niece" but that one does not have to. The consistent application of the "aunt" and "uncle" terms to the uncle's wife and aunt's husband, then, is in marked contrast to the alternate norms for the cousin's spouse, the nephew and niece's spouse, or the spouse's sibling's child's spouse.

Now let us turn the matter entirely around. Instead of asking about kinship terms, consider instead the terms that are used for persons who are, in one or another sense, relatives. Here again we can ask this question in the form in which American culture puts it: Who calls whom what?

Terms for relatives consist or kinship terms of some kind (mother, ma, pop, uncle, etc.), or nonkinship terms. Those which are not kinship terms are either names, words, or phrases (Jack, Smith, kid, mister, old man, the old lady, etc.). A third category is formed by combining the first two (Uncle Jack, Gramma Smith, Sister Sue).

The kinship terms themselves are of two kinds: the formal terms formally used, and the informal terms informally used. This second kind might also be described as "intimate" forms.[6] Thus, "father" is formal, "pa" is informal or intimate; "grandmother" is formal, "nanna" is informal.

The names, words, and phrases also divide in the same way into formal and informal or intimate forms. First names are informal and intimate as against formal last names. But first names can be formal or informal as well, so that John is the formal form, Johnny the informal form. Titles are formal; certain words and phrases are not. Mister and doctor are formal; old man and boss are not.

So much for "what." "Who" and "whom" divide into those who are equal and those who are not. Equal should not be confused with "the same." Brothers may be equal and the same; brother and sister may be equal but hardly the same.

Symmetrical usage is the mark of equality. Cousins who are equal may call each other by their first names, by nicknames, or by a combination of kinship term and first name (as in "Cousin Jane"). When two couples whose children have said that they intend to marry meet for the first time, if they consider themselves equal or wish to at least proceed on that manifest assumption, they may be introduced to each other and address each other symmetrically by their title-plus-last-name. Thus, they will be introduced as Mr. and Mrs. Lastname and call each other by that symmetrical form. Husband and wife may use pet names, terms of endearment, or the all-purpose "honey" or "dear," or they may, in a more Victorian context, use the formal Mr. and Mrs. or Doctor and Mrs. for each other, when they are treating each other as equals. It especially should be noted that two different formal terms may be symmetrical (or equal) but different, rather than being asymmetrical.

Asymmetrical usage is a mark of inequality. Where one person shows respect to the other, one is senior and the other junior, or one is superior and the other inferior, it marks distance between unequals. In asymmetrical usage the senior has the right to expect that the junior will use respectful forms while the senior has the right to use intimate, informal, personal forms.

The most obvious example is in parent–child usages. A father may address a son by the son's first name, but certain canons of propriety require the son to call him "father." A variant may be where the son calls the father "dad"; in another variant the father calls the son not by his

[6] See in this connection P. Friedrich, "Structural Implications of Russian Pronominal Usage," in *Sociolinguistics*, ed. W. Bright (The Hague: Mouton & Co., 1966), pp. 214-59. Also see R. Brown and M. Ford, "Address in American English," *Journal of Abnormal and Social Psychology*, 62 (1961), 275-385.

formal first name, "John," but by his nickname, "Jack." (This does not mean that the *only* way to mark respect for a senior is by the use of asymmetrical forms. Terminology may be symmetrical and respect may be paid in other coin.)

Other examples come readily to hand. Kinship-term-plus-first-name to first name is a common one. Here it may be Uncle John—James; Father John—Mary; Grandfather Jones—Susan; and so on. Each term in the equation can of course vary in the ways that have already been indicated above (grandfather, grandpa, grandpop, grandpappy, grampa, etc.).

In asymmetrical usages, it is the right of the superior to control any changes in the arrangement, and it is on the initiative of the superior that changes are properly made. As I have already noted, for instance, when a boy grows up and feels adult, and his mother's brother recognizes this state of affairs, he may suggest that he be called "Bill" now instead of the old "Uncle Bill"; or if his nephew tactfully tries it, he may give his permission for the change. When a mother-in-law suggests that she be called "Mary" instead of "Mrs. Jones" by her son-in-law, very much the same thing is happening. Here too the son-in-law may tactfully try it, but it is her right to permit it or not. The period of transition from the time when the potential son-in-law addresses her as "Mrs. Jones" to the time when she initiates the change to "Mary" may be occupied by a period of suspended address or no-naming, where the son-in-law is careful to avoid the "Mrs. Lastname" form as being entirely too formal and cumbersome, but has not yet had permission to use the informal, intimate first-name form.

The problematic data that require some explanation include the unanimity with which informants insist that the uncle's wife and the aunt's husband are "aunt" and "uncle," respectively. This requires some explanation, since relatives in comparable categories appear to be governed by alternate norms which make it a matter of personal option whether they are cousin, nephew, or niece. Since the latter kind of response from informants—that alternate norms govern this situation—is consistent with everything else that we know about the American kinship system, the data which are inconsistent and must be explained are, paradoxically enough, those about which informants are in almost complete agreement; namely, that uncle's wife is properly called "aunt," and that aunt's husband is properly called "uncle."

What these persons are called, what the proper kinship terms for them are, and in what terms they are thought of are distinct and different questions from how they are classed, or what kinds of persons they are. I have already indicated that at the level of kinds of persons, alternate norms govern their construction as relatives. This is a matter of choice between two forms: first, whether to count them as relatives in law, and second, whether not to count them as relatives at all.

What they are called, or the proper kinship terms for them, depends on who is calling them, as the formula which informants state puts it (Who calls whom what?). Kinship terms are used as status-equivalence and status-difference markers in that if the person calling them is junior to them, and the only link with them is that they are married to a blood relative, then they must be treated with respect, and the respectful form is asymmetrical. This form is the kinship term plus the first name. The older person is called "uncle" or "aunt" plus the first name, and the younger person is first-named in return.

Where the facts are inconsistent, however, the form changes. Where the person—whether he is the parent's sibling or the parent's sibling's spouse—can be regarded as an age equal, symmetrical first-naming is the proper form. Where the person—parent's sibling or parent's sibling's spouse—is in a warm, friendly, egalitarian relationship, symmetrical first-naming can be one of the proper forms. Where Ego is now mature and no longer a child and this fact is honored (rather than the fact that they are still considerably different in age, which may also be true), then symmetrical first-naming can be one of the proper forms. Where the person—parent's sibling or parent's sibling's spouse—is distant, hostile, not respected, then either antagonistic first-naming or no-naming may be the appropriate forms to mark the situation.

In summary, it is well to go back to the very first question posed in dealing with kinship terms in this chapter. Does it follow that an uncle's wife or an aunt's husband is counted as a relative *because* it is proper to call them "aunt" and "uncle," respectively? The answer is simple; no, it does not follow at all. Kinship terms are used as status markers in one of the special aspects of the more general rule that they mark a code for conduct, a pattern for behavior, a kind of relationship. Status difference or equivalence is simply one special kind of relationship between persons who may be in a kinship relationship as well. The relative as a person is not just somebody with whom a relationship of diffuse, enduring solidarity obtains. The relative as a person is made up of other elements as well. He may be equal or unequal by virtue of his age or some other attribute; he will be male or female; and so on. Where he is senior in some respect he requires respectful treatment, and the mark of respect for a parent's sibling's spouse is the use of kinship-term-plus-first-name forms, asymmetrically linked to the reciprocal first-name form; "Uncle Bill" and "John." [7]

[7] Compare F. G. Lounsbury, "Another View of the Trobriand Kinship Categories," in "Formal Semantic Analysis," ed. E. A. Hammel, *American Anthropologist*, 67:5, Part 2 (1965), 162-67; F. G. Lounsbury, "A Formal Account of the Crow- and Omaha-Type Kinship Terminologies," in *Explorations in Cultural Anthropology*, ed. W. H. Goodenough (New York: McGraw-Hill Book Company, 1964), footnote 21; and Goodenough, 1965, *op. cit.* Goodenough treats the uncle's wife and the aunt's husband as *necessarily* relatives by marriage. He recognizes but does not resolve a problem with the divorced or widowed uncle's, aunt's or grandparent's spouse. It is clear from his exposition that the cousin's spouse, the spouse of a nephew or niece, and the spouse of a spouse's nephew or niece are not included in the meanings of any of the kinship terms he lists nor are they considered to be relatives by marriage. As I have already indicated, his is certainly one of the alternate patterns which can be found in America and his data is, therefore, perfectly good as far as it goes. But on a theoretical level it is not clear why he fails to resolve the ambiguous status of the second or subsequent spouse of an aunt, uncle or grandparent and why he did not look further than his informants' flat statement that an aunt's husband and uncle's wife were *uncle* and *aunt* respectively, and that they were relatives by marriage. For it is clearly inconsistent for them to be *uncle* and *aunt* when cousin's spouse is not *cousin* and son's spouse is not *daughter*. What I have suggested above is, I suggest again explicitly here, particularly true for informants like Goodenough's. Uncle's wife is accorded *aunt* as a form of respect, aunt's husband is accorded *uncle* as a form of respect, and this form of respect along with the kinship role which is implied are enforced on children who, when they reach the age of consent if not before, may simply slip the relationship and the forms implicitly, if not openly, and terminate the relationship. Simply put, therefore, Goodenough's is an ethnographic error in that he failed to elicit *all* of the relevant information and a theoretical error in that he failed to integrate *all* of the relevant information into his theoretical constructs. The inclusion of the kintypes MoSiHu, FaSiHu under the kinship term *uncle* and MoBrWi and FaBrWi under the kinship term *aunt* without further qualification or explanation is an ethnographic error which seems dictated by the theory of componential analysis, not by the full weight of the information which could be elicited from his informant. Precisely this same criticism must be directed at Lounsbury as well, for he never finds out from his informants whether indeed the step-kin rule is an ethnographic fact of the culture he is analysing or a theoretical distortion which he is imposing on the ethnographic facts.

CHAPTER SIX

Conclusion

The relationship between man and nature in American culture is an active one. It is not aimed at a balance between opposed forces, for it is not deemed to be man's place to accept the fate which nature has defined for him. Instead, it is man's place to dominate nature, to control it, to use nature's powers for his own ends. Whether this is done by the prevention and cure of illness, the bridging of great rivers, or the conquest of space does not matter. In American culture man's fate is seen as one which follows the injunction, Master Nature! His science and technology and much of his life is devoted to that task.

But at home things are different. Where kinship and family are concerned, American culture appears to turn things topsy-turvy. For this is one part of nature with which man has made his peace and in terms of which he is content to find his fate. What is out there in nature, say the definitions of American culture, is what kinship is. Kinship is the blood relationship, the fact of shared biogenetic substance. Kinship is the mother's bond of flesh and blood with her child, and her maternal instinct is her love for it. This is nature; these are natural things; these are the ways of nature. To be otherwise is unnatural, artificial, contrary to nature.

Yet in American culture man is defined as being very much a part of nature, obeying the laws of nature just like everything else. The antithesis of the first paragraph is thus denied in the second. Yet both paragraphs are true of American culture, and both represent American culture in very important ways.

Although I have put this set of contradictions in the most general terms and at the most general level, the same contradictions occur at the level of very specific matters between kinship and the rest of American culture.

Sexuality in American culture is a case in point. Of all of the forms of sexuality of which human beings are capable, only one is legitimate and proper according to the standards of American culture, and that is heterosexual relations, genital to genital, between man and wife. All other forms are improper and held to be morally wrong. (See footnote 3, Chapter Three.)

Man is thus faced with an array of possibilities in his own nature which he must master. He should control them, so that he determines their fate; they should not be free to determine his fate.

Yet heterosexual relations, genital to genital, between husband and wife, are defined as the natural state of affairs, the way it is, and the way it should be. As the state of nature itself, it *is* marriage. And it is good, gratifying, rewarding. As I said above, quoting what I believe is the culturally stated maxim, It should *be* fun, but is not *for* fun. Indeed, anything else, in any other way, and with any other aim, is defined in American culture as unnatural.

The antithesis between man and nature is resolved at the very next level by the premise that man is only one special part of nature. But if man is viewed as being a part of nature, then the antithesis arises at a quite different level of American culture. This antithesis becomes one between two opposed parts of nature itself, one of which is defined in American culture as animal, and the other of which is human (or man). What is distinctly human, as against animal, is reason or intelligence. But intelligence is not something off by itself, existing alone and apart from everything else. It is a part of nature, and it is an attribute of that part of nature which American culture defines as animal. Thus again the antithesis between man and animal is resolved at the very next level by the premise that man is but one special kind of animal, and his intelligence is but a special kind of animal intelligence. Man's is the capacity to reason, the premise of American culture has it, against animal's unreason.

And so another contradiction emerges. For human reason or intelligence, it seems clearly given in American culture, departs from what is animal in nature, and thereby departs at the same time from what is natural. Reason selects the good and rejects the bad in nature, and reason invents ways, customs, rules, laws.

American culture postulates a direct relationship between the extent to which intelligence has acted and the distance of the product from the state of nature. To put this somewhat differently, the more that human reason has worked at it, the less of nature there is left. The effect of reason and intelligence is described as being "cultivated," "sophisticated," "artificial," "unnatural." [1]

At whatever level it is taken, then, there remains a contradiction between man and nature. It is either man against nature directly (as in man's fight against disease), man as a part of nature against the animal part of nature (as in sexuality), or man's reason against unreasoning animal nature.

The contradiction between the good and the bad parts of nature, as they are contained in man as an animal and as a part of nature himself, and the contradiction between the fact that if a man departs too far from nature nothing but bad (unnatural) can result are resolved by the order of law.

According to the postulates of American culture the order of law is the outcome of the action of human reason on nature. The good is selected, discovered, chosen; rules and regulations (the order of law) are established to maintain and perpetuate the good. Whether this is at the level of discovering the cure or prevention of a disease or routinizing (by rules) the cure or prevention of that disease does not matter. But it can also be done in another way, and that is by inventing some customary or proper way of behaving. Rules are made, in the sense of invented, for just this purpose. And so government is regarded in American culture as the formulator of laws and rules in the light of reason.

The anthropologist's notion of culture is thus not very different from the American's notion of the order of law. This being so, it is not a matter of culture *against* nature, nor of culture *against* man at all. In America, it is the order of law, that is, culture, which resolves the contradictions between man and nature, which are contradictions within nature itself.

I suggest that it is within the framework of American culture itself that American kinship as a cultural system is best understood. So it is that in one sense "family" in American culture *is* simply the natural biological state of affairs centering on reproduction. Marriage, in its most limited sense, *is* sexual union. The reproducing pair, living together with their offspring, *is* the family.

But however natural this is, it is not distinguished in any way from the animal, and this, of course, is why Americans see a pair of wolves with their pups in their cave as a family.

It is the order of law, based on reason, which at once distinguishes the

[1] "Unnatural" is thus used to mean both far from nature, contrived, without any basis in nature, and also that part of nature which is wrong, bad, evil, or repulsive to human reason as in the "unnatural" sexual acts.

human from the animal, yet keeps it all within the realm of nature and based on nature. This comes about when reason regulates, when human sensibilities define the proper kind of sexual union from among all possible kinds, when human intelligence chooses and defines the proper kind of behavior between genitor and offspring. For then there is the mastery of nature through nature's own laws, humanly selected and intelligently ordered, which constitutes the ideal of American culture. It is the order of law, based on reason and on nature, which, combined with nature, is the most powerful and the most nearly ideal arrangement in the definition of American culture.

The classification of relatives in American kinship is built on the same set of premises set in the same relationship to each other. The relative in nature is at one extreme, the relative in law is at the other extreme. The first is but a relationship of nature, fundamental as that is. The second is but a set of artificial rules or regulations for conduct, without substantive or natural base. But the blood relative, related in nature and by law, brings together the best of nature modified by human reason; he is thus the relative in the truest and most highly valued sense.[2]

II.

I have put the relations between man and nature as they are defined in American culture as a set of contradictions which are resolved in various ways. But the different relations between man and nature can be stated in another way which is equally true but has somewhat different significance.

The formal category of nature, as it is defined in American culture, includes within it both man and animal. Yet in another context, the meaning of the word "man" is sharply differentiated from the category of nature and set apart from it.

This pattern is the same as that for the category "relative," where the word is used to include anyone related by blood or marriage in one meaning, and where on the other hand the word is reserved for blood

---

[2] I have already discussed other sets of contradictions and their resolutions which crosscut those I have focused on in this section: the contradiction set in terms of place between work and home, resolved by the vacation; and the contradiction set in terms of code for conduct between family (or kinship) and work, resolved by friendship. These two contradictions in turn distinguish between substance and action, between physical nature as objective and action as subjective. This distinction seems systematically elaborated throughout all of American culture. Just as substance and code for conduct are distinct in American kinship, so too work as a place and work as a form of activity are distinct. Sometimes this distinction is marked by grammatical form, as with friend and friendship, kin and kinship, relative and relationship. But this is not always so—take work, which is both place and activity.

relatives alone and juxtaposed to in-laws. I reported this above as the situation in which it is equally possible for a person to say that his wife (or husband) is a relative because she (or he) is an in-law, and to say that his wife (or husband) is *not* a relative because she (or he) is an in-law.

The very same pattern occurs with the term "family," which can mean both the unit of husband, wife, and child and the aggregation of all those who are relatives, or can be reserved for the unit of husband, wife, and child alone.

The category of blood follows this pattern too. It not only means the red stuff which courses through the veins, but also that combination of substance and code for conduct which those who share that red stuff, the blood relatives, should have. In one sense its meaning is reserved to that of substance, in the other it includes both substance and law.

Of course, each of the kinship terms for blood relatives follows this pattern too, so that "father" is both the genitor and the father role or its meaning is restricted to genitor alone.

So too the notion of distance can be physical, socioemotional, and genealogical, as against its restricted meaning as genealogical alone.

Finally, the most important example is the fundamental distinction in American kinship between the relative as a person and the distinctive features which define the person as a relative. These constitute two major systems, the one restricted to a set of distinctive features, defined and differentiated by a single symbol, and the other, the personification in actable terms of a variety of different symbol systems, including the first.

In restating this pattern from that of a set of contradictions with a resolution to that of a system of marked and unmarked categories [3] which interlock and overlap, it is not my intention to now deny that in some important respect these are indeed also contradictions, and that they are in fact resolved in the ways suggested. But it should be clear that they are, at the same time, cultural categories whose value, marked and unmarked, is equally true.

Indeed, the fact that these exist *both* as a system of contradictions and their resolution, *and* as a system of marked and unmarked categories in American kinship as a cultural system is the crucial fact. For it is precisely this fact which makes it possible to solve what I regard as the fundamental and most difficult problem in the analysis of American kin-

---

[3] J. Greenberg, *Language Universals* (The Hague: Mouton & Co., 1966). I have based my discussion on Greenberg's development of the concept of marked/unmarked categories.

ship. This is the problem presented by the great range of variation at almost every level.

I say "almost every level" because at one level, that of the distinctive features, there is no variance, while at all other levels the variance is great.

The first step in solving the problem of variance in the American kinship system consists of recognizing that there are really two systems operating, and that the two are closely articulated but by no means identical.

Or, to put it in operational terms, the first step in solving the problem of variance in the American kinship system consists in *listening to the informants*.

At first informants make what the listener can only interpret as noise. But soon the noise changes to what can best be described as double-talk. Informants seem incapable of using words precisely, of saying what they mean or meaning what they say. The listener who believes that words have precise, clearly defined and standardized meanings finds this intensely frustrating. The subtle manipulations that go on when the words "relative," "related," and "relationship" are used are particularly taxing. This is true for every word used in connection with kinship, from such simple notions as "distance" through the kinship terms, such as "uncle" and "aunt."

But it soon becomes clear that the double-talk of the informants is nothing more than the same words, now in their marked, now in their unmarked meanings; the informants themselves are not fully aware of the fact that they shift usages, sometimes in the middle of a sentence. Thus some informants may start a sentence with the word "mother," meaning genetrix, and end by using "mother" as a verb.

The first step, then, consists in making the distinction between the relative as a person and the distinctive features which define the person as a relative. This simply separates the system of distinctive features from the system of person-centered definitions.

That this first step is valid is shown not only by the fact that the data themselves easily divide in this way, but more importantly by the fact that once the distinction is made it can be seen that there is no variance where the distinctive features are concerned; all the variance occurs with regard to the person-centered system. The presence or absence of variance is thus a distinguishing mark of the two systems.

The variance which is associated with the person-centered system is of two different kinds. One consists of the fact that the immediate data which the observer encounters are specific decisions persons have made about specific people under special circumstances where the system itself permits a wide variety of alternate modes of legitimate action. I have already developed this point in detail in Chapters IV and V and it is sufficient to simply repeat here that this array of diverse data depends in part on the fact that the different words and categories of American kinship each have a number of different meanings (polysemy); that these different meanings may distribute as marked and unmarked categories, or as contradictions and resolutions; and that the actor is free to choose which of the many meanings in this array he will employ.

The second kind of variance is at the level of the different normative constructs of the relative as a person. The fundamental question which this kind of variance raises is the one I posed in the Introduction, namely, whether there is a single American kinship system, with perhaps variant forms associated with one or another ethnic, religious, class, or regional group, or whether there are really many different kinship systems, which are all simply held together by the framework of the United States as a geographic and political unit.

The answer now seems clear. The system of distinctive features, defined and differentiated in terms of one central symbol, constitutes a firm, fixed core which provides the defining feature for every kind of person. It is around these fixed features that variation occurs, and at least in this sense it can be said that there is a single American kinship system.[4]

There is another reason for saying that there is one system, not many: The variant forms of the normative definitions of the different kinds of relatives as persons also constitute a single system of variation and not a series of *ad hoc* or random variants.

This conclusion is based partly on the premise that the different components of the normative definition of the relative as a person have a definite order and are integrated in accordance with some clear value hierarchy.[5]

Every normative construct of a relative as a person starts with the fixed, distinctive features. Thus a father is in the first instance the genitor, and as a relative or member of the family he is guided by considerations of enduring, diffuse solidarity or love.

But the father as a person has a class position, and he is of the male

[4] Whether the system is even wider and more extensive than American culture alone must remain an open, empirical question at this time.

[5] I have not developed this point systematically in this book. Neither have I presented any systematic treatment of the problem of just which components, from which symbol systems other than kinship, go to make up the normative definition of the relative as a person in American culture. What follows, therefore, must be taken with more than the usual grain of salt; it is at best a programmatic statement which may prove useful when it is worked out fully.

sex. How do these components distribute themselves? Maleness is varied by class position. What is appropriate and proper for a male upper-class person who is a father is different from the standards appropriate for a male middle-class person who is a father. These in turn are not the same as the standards for the behavior of a male lower-class person who is a father.

In a very important sense, then, variation in what has been called "family form" consists of variation at the level of the family as a group of persons and variation in the normative definition of the relative as a member of the family.

Such variation, in turn, does not depend on variation in the kinship component; that is fixed and standard, since it consists of the distinctive features. Such variation depends instead on variables such as sex-role differentiation from the sex-attribute system, and class differentiation from the stratification system. Variation in family form, then, is largely a matter of variation in class and sex-role attribute, not kinship or family, and should be studied as such.

It is precisely because a single-core system of kinship is the central component of every normative definition of the relative as a person that it is possible to say that there is a single kinship system for the United States. And it is for the very same reason that the variant and variable normative definitions can be regarded as part of one system, not many systems. For the sex-attribute or sex-role-differentiation system has its own set of distinctive features, which consitutes a single system in American culture. The stratification system also is part of a single system.

III.

I turn now to the question of sexual intercourse as the central symbol of American kinship as a cultural system.

It will be helpful to begin with a few simple distinctions. First, sexual intercourse can be seen as a set of *biological facts*. These are part of the world. They exist, and they have effects.

Second, there are certain cultural notions and constructs *about* biological facts. The example *par excellence* in American culture is the life-sciences—biology, zoology, biochemistry, and so on. This is a cultural system explicitly attuned to those biological facts as such. It discovers them, studies them, organizes what it regards as facts into a system. But it remains a system of cultural constructs which should not be confused with the biological facts themselves. Outside the formal organization of the sciences there are also cultural notions and beliefs *about* biological facts. In certain respects both the formal science and the informal ethnoscience are the same. Both may in fact be in error in some matters, both may in fact be correct in some matters, but both serve as guides for the actions of people dealing in some way with those biological facts. In addition, both are organized so as to remain attuned to the biological facts themselves; that is, both are models of the reality which consists of the *biological facts*. Hence there is a very strong tendency—though this is far from perfectly carried out—to adjust the culture *to* the facts and not vice versa, and to change the cultural constructs when they fail to conform with the facts. This is seldom a perfect process for many reasons which need not detain us here.

Third, there are certain cultural notions which are put, phrased, expressed, symbolized by cultural notions *depicting* biological facts, or what purport to be biological facts. Sexual intercourse and the attendant elements which are said to be biological facts *insofar as they concern kinship* as a cultural system, are of this order. Kinship is *not* a theory about biology; but biology serves to formulate a theory about kinship.

A much simpler example to start with than sexual intercourse, however, is the matter of the heart; its loss, its breaking, its swelling, and its feeling.

First, there is the heart, a biological fact. Second, there is a body of science and ethnoscience about the heart—that it pumps blood and has four chambers and so on. And third, there is that heartbreaking moment when a man loses his heart to the girl of his dreams, who jilts him, thus really breaking his heart. Or she may not jilt him, and his heart will swell with pride and joy, while he pleads his suit—from the heart, of course—in a way which he hopes will be taken as heartfelt. Heartfelt, in just the same way as when he puts his right hand (or his hat) over his heart as the American flag goes by during a parade, or when he pledges allegiance to the American flag.

This is not a set of biological facts. Neither is it a theory *about* biological facts, and no amount of research about the heart has had any effect on this particular collection of cultural constructs depicting the heart. Whether these ever were regarded as biological facts, whether the seat of the emotions was once believed to be the biological organ, does not really matter now.

But the heart is a very good example because it is such a poor example. There is a world of difference to the native between the biological fact of the heart and the idea of a heartache or broken heart. The heart in this context is a metaphor at best, and everyone who uses it in that way knows that it is a metaphor. The simple distinction between heartache and heartburn brings this metaphorical quality out quite clearly, for the former *stands for* an emotional state, the latter *is* purely gastric and quite somatic. In American culture, kinship *is* biology; the broken heart and heartache are not.

So much of kinship and family in American culture is defined as being nature itself, required by nature, or directly determined by nature that it is quite difficult, often impossible, in fact, for Americans to see this as a set of cultural constructs and not the biological facts themselves. They see the facts of flesh and blood as the pertinent facts, the facts which contain the actual identity of parent and child, which contain the force which compels the deep feeling and love between the two, and which make them "only natural." "The milk of human kindness" is a metaphor for Americans, but it is not an empty metaphor like the heart. For without the milk, kindly given, hardly a child would survive.

These biological facts, the biological prerequisites for human existence, exist and remain. The child does not live without the milk of human kindness, both as nourishment and as protection. Nor does the child come into being except by the fertilized egg which, except for those rare cases of artificial insemination, is the outcome of sexual intercourse. These are biological facts. They are facts of life and facts of nature.

There is also a system of constructs in American culture about those biological facts. That system exists in an adjusted and adjustable relationship with the biological facts.

But these same cultural constructs which depict these biological facts have another quality. They have as one of their aspects a symbolic quality, which means that they represent something other than what they are, over and above and in addition to their existence as biological facts and as cultural constructs about biological facts. They serve in this respect as symbols precisely because there is no necessary or intrinsic relationship between them and what they symbolize.

What, then, do the cultural constructs depicting the facts of sexual intercourse symbolize?

They symbolize diffuse, enduring solidarity. They symbolize those kinds of interpersonal relations which human beings as biological beings *must* have if they are to be born and grow up. They symbolize trust, but a special kind of trust which is not contingent and which does not depend on reciprocity. They stand for the fact that birth survives death, and that solidarity *is* enduring. And they stand for the fact that man can create, by his own act and as an act of will, and is not simply an object of nature's mindless mercy.

In just the same way that reproduction is a set of biological facts that is prerequisite to the continuity of a society as a body of people, so too, diffuse, enduring solidarity is a social and psychobiological prerequiste to the continuity of both the society and its culture.

But how can this be expressed? How can it be said? How can it be put so that it can guide the actions and show the paths for people to follow? If these things somehow need to be done, what rules need to be set to assure that they are done, for people do not have the instinctive patterns of ants. They need to learn what they like to think are their instincts. And so a model is needed, a model to live by.

What better model than sexual intercourse and its attendant psycho-biological elements? These biological facts are transformed by the attribution of meaning into cultural constructs and they then constitute a model for *commitment,* for the passionate attachment which is one side of trust, and for the unreasoning and unreasonable set of conditions which alone make "solidarity" really solidary, and make it both enduring and diffuse.

CHAPTER SEVEN

Twelve Years Later

I.

This book, completed in 1967, published in 1968, and reprinted in 1980, marks an important point in a larger enterprise. It represents my first major piece of work on two long-standing interests: the study of American culture and the development of a theory of culture. Its special significance, for me, is that it brings together both of these interests in their traditional and proper balance, making use of an explicit theory of culture in the analysis of a concrete body of data. Theory without data and data without theory are inconceivable to me, for the one always entails the other. It is easy to see the implicit theory in any work that purports to be pure description; it is harder to see the implicit body of data around which a theory develops, but it is there nonetheless.

This enterprise goes back to my graduate student days. My interest in studying American culture started in the early 1940s, and my interest in developing a theory of culture which could accord with Talcott Parsons's theory of social action started when I returned to graduate school in 1946 after World War II. I can claim no speed record. And it is not unreasonable to say that from those years of effort there has come forth a very small book indeed.

As I reported in "What is Kinship all About," I realized too late that the title of the book was wrong, for I found that I had much more than American kinship by the tail. The book was in a sense more about certain fundamental postulates of American culture in general than it was about "kinship." What was most annoying about this was that I had been telling myself (and anyone who had the patience to listen) for a long time that there was no such thing as "kinship," that it was a chimera, an artifact of a bad theory. To get hoist in this way was, and remains, acutely embarassing.

Realizing that I was dealing with more than American "kinship," I immediately wrote "Kinship, Nationality and Religion in American Culture" which, in effect, said that what I had been calling "kinship" really also encompassed at least nationality and religion in American culture. Not only was the domain of "kinship" not distinct in American culture, it was also the way into a much larger domain that I happened, for good historical reasons, to get started on. A short paper, "American Kin Categories," for the Levi-Strauss Festschrift followed. Then, working with Raymond T. Smith, the focus shifted to a lower class group of Blacks, Latinos, and Appalachians in Chicago, and on the basis of this new body of data, a first draft of a new book was written in 1970, entirely revised, and published in 1973 as *Class Differences and Sex Roles in American Kinship and Family Structure.*

Meanwhile, in 1972, the paper "What is Kinship all About" attempted to bring the lessons of this book to the more general problem of the anthropological study of "kinship." That is, by reviewing the theoretical position of this book and contrasting it with the more orthodox theory generally held, I tried to show that "kinship" as a thing, as an object of study, was at best only possible in a very restricted sense, and then probably only in Western cultures such as that in the United States. This is the more conservative, temperate statement of the message of that paper. The more dramatic statement was that "kinship" was, like totemism, a non-subject, and purely an artifact of a demonstrably false theory. Needless to say, this message was not received with universal acclaim and the anthropological profession did not pour into the streets in joyous celebration. One lesson of this paper is that it is much more painful to disagree than it is to be wrong. None of this diminishes the paper in my own estimation. I think that it is a compelling position.

While that paper was brewing, James Boon and I were talking of Levi-Strauss's structuralism and the differences in Levi-Strauss's treatment of kinship and myth. This talk resulted in the first draft of "Kinship vis-à-vis Myth," which we gave at one of the annual meetings of the American Anthropological Association. But again, all my contribution to that paper derived in more or less direct form from the implications of *American Kinship,* and so it, too, represented merely another development of the theory first stated most clearly in *American Kinship.*

In late 1968 and in 1969, the analysis of the genealogies we had collected along with all the other material on which this book is based was begun in earnest, but work had to be suspended in the early 1970s, although the draft version was fairly complete by 1972. Thus, *The American Kin Universe* did not appear until 1975.

Keith Basso and Henry Selby had arranged a conference sponsored by the School for American Research in Santa Fe in March of 1974 where they and Ira Buchler, Susan Ervin-Tripp, Roy d'Andrade, Clifford Geertz, Ellie Maranda, Harold Scheffler, Michael Silverstein, and I spent endless, and for me intensely happy, hours, discussing *Meaning in Anthropology*, exactly what I thought my theory of culture was about. My debt to all of them is considerable, for I learned much from them, and faster than I might have otherwise. "Notes Toward a Theory of Culture" appears in the volume resulting from that conference.

And so it goes. I read a paper in June 1977 at a Smithsonian Institution symposium called "Kinship, Community and Locality in American Culture" which has just been published. During the late 1960s, I began to rework some of my Yap material in terms of a better developed theory of culture, and it will come as no surprise that its center of interest is Yap "kinship." I gave an early and abbreviated version of this paper to the Anthropology Department of the University of New Mexico as one of the Fred Harvey, Jr. Lectures in 1976, but this has grown into another book which should be completed soon (Schneider forthcoming).

Thus *American Kinship* is part of a larger body of work that still continues and still focuses on the problem of culture theory based on data from the study of American "kinship," Yap, and the Mescalero Apache, even when data from one or another of these cultures is not explicitly cited.

Finally, two points should be clarified for the record. First, the opposition between "substance" and "code" or "code for conduct," which was first set forth in detail in this book has been picked up and applied to some other cultures by other anthropologists, including some working on materials from India. So far as I am concerned this opposition is demonstrably important in American culture. If it turns out to be useful in the analysis of materials from India or elsewhere, good. But I myself make only one limited claim for this opposition; it is an important part of American culture. I make no claims for its universality, generality, or applicability anywhere else.

The second point is rather like the first. So far as I am concerned, "diffuse, enduring solidarity" is a fundamental feature of certain areas of American culture. Since I have taken the clear position that I do not believe that the concept of "kinship" in general is useful, and that I believe that "kinship" as a universal is false, and that it is a non-problem, it would be absurd of me to claim that "diffuse, enduring solidarity" is characteristic of "kinship" in general. For me, at this moment, there is only American "kinship" and even that is very limited in its definition. Hence the attempt that has been made, by Craig for example, to equate "diffuse, enduring solidarity" with Professor Meyer Fortes's concept of the "axiom of amity" is, to put it politely, misguided. To treat a specific characteristic of one particular culture as a feature of a fictive universal hardly seems wise to me. All I mean by "diffuse, enduring solidarity" is a feature of American culture. If Dr. Craig should decline to agree with me and insist that one can indeed discuss "kinship" in general, as a universal feature of every culture, and thereby draw parallels between Fortes's "axiom of amity" and my "diffuse, enduring solidarity" that is entirely his affair. But my point remains the same; the only claim that I make for "diffuse, enduring solidarity" is for the place that I have described for it in American culture.

II.

The work on which *American Kinship* was based was done using almost entirely white, urban, middle class informants. I tried to expand my horizons by reading as much as I could in the sociological literature about lower class family and kinship and also spent more hours than proved useful looking for ethnic and "race" differences as well. In retrospect, it was time that had to be wasted. To have failed to comb the literature would have been grave dereliction of scholarly duty. But having done so, precious little came of it. Endless tirades and agonized reviews of the state of marriage and divorce never touched those crucial questions—or questions crucial to me—namely, How is marriage to be understood? How is it defined? Instead I learned that some felt marriage was doomed and others felt that the family, and hence marriage, was the cornerstone of all civilization as we know it, and that the rising rate of divorce was either ghastly or commendable. But none of the scholarly works I consulted told me very much about what I wanted to know. And most important was the fact that the whole family and kinship system of the United States was treated in terms of the white, urban, middle class. Earlier, Margaret Mead, among others, tried to make the case that the middle class set the standard, stated the aspired goals, formulated the values which permeated every other strata of American society. Therefore white, urban, middle class values could legitimately be taken to represent the cultural norms. It is ironic that it took the civil rights movement, not systematic scientific enquiry, to dispel that comforting bit of ethnocentricity. (Since the upper class has not entered into or initiated any Upper Class Rights Movement we are still very much in the dark about what goes on there.)

But the long and the short of it was that I did make some very bad mistakes, and these came out most clearly when Raymond T. Smith and I studied some Chicago Blacks, Latinos, and Appalachians, all of whom were lower class. The results of this study have now been reprinted by the University of Michigan Press as *Class Differences in American Kinship* (1978). See Barnett and Silverman in this connection.

In the first place, my claim that there is only one American kinship system tripped over the fact that the "family" means something different to the lower class from what it does to the middle class. Family and household have been persistently confused in the ethnographic literature. This may be a consequence of the fact that most ethnographers are middle class and the middle class tends to treat the family and the household as one and the same thing. The lower class does not. Co-residence is not nearly the great symbol of unity for the lower class family that it is for the middle class. So there are some corrections in *Class Differences in American Kinship* of statements in *American Kinship*. Many of these corrections sort out that which applies to all Americans from what is class-linked. But most of what was said in *American Kinship* survives. One of its most useful aspects is that *American Kinship* did, perhaps impetuously, offer some hypotheses which the later research could deal with explicitly and, where necessary, correct. One of these corrections is the idea that the "family" and co-residence of the middle class is identical to the "family" and co-residence of the lower class. There are a number of other, perhaps less serious errors which the later book corrects, but this is one of the major ones.

A second error which later research has corrected is the assertion that ethnicity does not matter, that once an ethnic group is in the United States, it takes over American culture, lock, stock, and barrel, and so I felt free to talk about American "kinship" as applying equally to different ethnic groups. Sylvia Yanagisako showed that this was not true for Japanese-Americans, and in an unpublished paper, Phyllis Chock suggests tactfully that it would be stretching the case to claim that Greek-Americans are just exactly like all other Americans so far as their kinship system, as a cultural system, goes. I suspect that if our material were richer on the Latinos it would show some important differences, too.

The problem that remains is to see how each of these qualifications relates to the other and how the qualifications relate to the whole conception. It is not impossible that the variations in class and ethnicity are but systematic transformations of an underlying or more general set of similarities, and it may yet be shown that there is a single, coherent, and integrated pattern of which that part outlined in *American Kinship* is but one. Whatever the outcome of such an analysis, this raises the question of the integration of culture as I have defined it, and whether it can or cannot be regarded as more or less perfectly integrated.

The discussion above about data brings up the criticism that it contained little if any data at all. What is at issue, of course, is: Just what are data? For some, they apparently consist of a set of objectively verifiable facts which can be discovered and reported as pure description and which can and must be kept sharply distinct from any analysis or interpretations. My own position (as I have suggested above) is that the distinction between fact and analysis cannot be made sharply; that they are so interwoven they cannot be separated. Hence the presentation of what purports to be pure data is always a selection; that selection is always guided by implicit or explicit presuppositions, and those presuppositions form a more or less coherent theory. A set of facts or body of data is simply some empirical statement made within the framework of a conceptual scheme or theory, however inexplicit this remains. What I believe I have presented in *American Kinship* are "data" in this sense, just as it is "analysis" in the same sense.

This is not to deny that the six thousand pages of typed interview material (see p. 12) on which this book is largely based is not quite the same thing as this book. But even if one were to argue that those six thousand pages are the data and this book is the interpretation, it would be extraordinarily difficult to show that the material that went into the six thousand pages was not selected, and that its selection was not guided by very much the same theoretical considerations as guided its distillation into the one hundred and seventeen pages which constitute the book. Moreover, it is impossible to stipulate precisely the operations which transformed the six thousand pages of typed material into the one hundred seventeen which purport to represent it. The least that can be said is that there is indeed an intimate and determinate connection between the six thousand pages and the hundred and seventeen.

This is not the place to present a fully developed argument for the position I have taken. But it is the place to indicate why I cannot seriously accept this criticism as it stands. The fact remains that this book is largely in the form of generalizations, and the six thousand pages of field notes are specific instances, however formed by the apprehension, comprehension, and presuppositions of the field workers as reworked by the author. I could indeed have documented a series of extended examples for each of the generalizations made in this book. I have chosen, however, not to do so.

Here a piece of history is useful. At the time the manuscript was being written, a close associate went through the interviews and the observations and selected a veritable treasure trove of quotations from informants and of observations by field workers which "supported" almost every statement contained in *American Kinship*. It was a long, arduous task, and required a good knowledge of what I was writing and a detailed grasp of every bit of the huge mass of material collected in the field.

The well known rule that "no good deed goes unpunished" came into play. I took this collection of quotations and statements and read them over carefully. They did indeed provide support for all of the important points in the book and most of the minor ones as well. Here was an embarrassment of riches. But since data and analysis are inextricably intertwined, it is a direct corollary that statements by informants, quotations of what the natives actually said, observations about what they actually do can constitute nothing more than examples, or illustrations, and can in no sense be regarded as proving anything. To add this rich harvest of quotations to the book would, then, serve no purpose other than illustration, and might easily be misunderstood as confirming the analysis. On the one hand, I did not feel that a seriously undertaken work of the sort I thought I was doing needed illustrations to pep it up or give it a "feel for the data"; on the other hand, I wanted to be very, very sure that no one could possibly misinterpret what I was doing by being misled into thinking that the mere illustrations or examples could "prove" anything, or lend factual support for any interpretation. And if there were a choice between these two reasons for omitting almost all such illustrations, quotations, etc., it was the second reason I found most compelling. I have frequently been offended by other anthropologists, sociologists and psychologists who play what I think of as the questionable game of suggesting that their generalization is "proven" or "supported" by some appropriately chosen excerpt from the field materials.

I therefore omitted, except for a very few instances, the vast body of material that my associate had laboriously collected on the pious ground that I refused to cheat. I might be wrong in my analysis, but I was certainly not going to cheat. And using nice little quotes and convincing little illustrations was, I thought then and think equally strongly now, a form of cheating: it pretends to documentation when it is not that at all. Needless to say, my associate disagrees and has not forgiven me to this day.

So the only reasonable reply that I can make to those who hold that the book presents no data is to say simply, "The book is the data." I cannot expect everyone to agree with me, but I hope that my position is clear.

Of great interest to me, and I hope to readers of this book, are a series of closely interwoven problems that arise out of a theory of culture which centers on problems of meaning.

The best way into this area is by way of a short paragraph which Clifford Geertz published and which I have chosen to treat as being of direct concern to the theory of culture to which I have committed myself. Geertz says:

> Culture is most effectively treated, the argument goes, purely as a symbolic system (the catch phrase is, "in its own terms"), by isolating its elements, specifying the internal relationships among those elements, and then characterizing the whole system in some general way—according to the core symbols around which it is organized, the underlying structures of which it is a surface expression, or the ideological principles upon which it is based . . . this hermetical approach to things seems to me to run the danger (and increasingly to have been overtaken by it) of locking cultural analysis away from its proper object, the informal logic of actual life.
>
> Behavior must be attended to, and with some exactness, because it is through the flow of behavior—or more precisely, social action—that cultural forms find articulation. They find it as well, of course, in various sorts of artifacts, and various states of consciousness; but these draw their meaning from the role they play (Wittgenstein would say their 'use') in an ongoing pattern of life, not from any intrinsic relationships they bear to one another (Geertz, C., 1973, *The Interpretation of Cultures*, p. 17).

There is, in this brief quotation, a veritable mare's nest of problems, each of which has been put to me in one way or another as a criticism of *American Kinship.*

First, there is the problem of the relationship between culture treated as a system of symbols and meanings and what Geertz here calls "behavior—or more precisely social action." He uses Talcott Parsons's terms, and I presume that he uses Parsons's definition of them, too. Social action is behavior that is symbolically and meaningfully entailed, the symbols and meanings deriving from the shared system of symbols and meanings in a society. Behavior is the residual category; it is any action that is not entailed in the symbol and meaning system of a society—it is raw behavior, so to speak, not *social* action.

The Parsonian frame takes social action as the object of its study and it distinguishes four systems as the determinants of social action no one of which can be reduced to any other. These are, as is well known, the cultural, the social, the psychological, and the biological. Thus, elements from each of these systems are present in any concrete social action.

There is always a social component, always a psychological component, always a biological component, and always a cultural component in any social act.

As I tried to explain in "Notes Toward a Theory of Culture," I have taken Parsons's scheme (not his whole theory, but only this particular part of it) one step further than he has himself. If the cultural system, as he calls it, cannot be reduced to any other system of determinants of social action, and if indeed it does have systematic features, then two questions can be asked. One can ask the "proper Parsonian" question, What is the role that culture plays in social action? or, in other words, What is the effect of culture on social action in its determinant aspects? Further, one can ask, Wherein lie the systematic features of culture? In what way does it constitute a system? How are its elements related to each other? To put it in Geertz's terms, culture can be treated "purely as a symbolic system (the catch phrase is, 'in its own terms')."

But it is not necessary to be a "proper Parsonian." My position converges with the position of a number of other workers who are in no way Parsonian. If, however, one accepts Parsons's distinction between behavior and action it follows that since not all behavior is symbolically or meaningfully engaged (which is by itself a fair enough position), the symbolic part or the meaningfulness of action is an aspect of that behavior which indeed can legitimately be abstracted. This is no more than to say that if the abstractions are made with respect to their relations to each other, the system of abstractions can be studied in its own terms apart from the flow of action and with respect to the relations among the abstracted elements.

Saussure distinguished between *langue* and *parole;* Chomsky between competence and performance; Silverstein between function$_2$ and function$_1$; Sahlins in a recent, unpublished paper "Individual Experience and Cultural Order," between culture-as-constituted and culture-in-action or culture-as-lived.

I am well aware of the fact that there has been a great plundering of linguistics to find concepts and ideas which can be applied (all too often naively) to culture. I am also aware that language is often not the best analogy to culture and therefore the methods for its study cannot always be applied directly to the study of culture. But this is not an all or nothing matter. The problem is to apply the analogy where it is appropriate, and in this particular respect I think it applies. The fact that it converges in certain important respects with the Parsonian position can be taken as a good omen or a bad omen depending on one's outlook.

Where one denies the legitimacy of the study of *langue*, of competence, of Silverstein's function$_2$, one also denies the legitimacy of the study of culture-as-constituted. If we simply change "culture" to "language," some would deny that language-as-constituted can be a proper object of study and that it can be studied only as it is actually spoken. Grammar, syntax, vocabulary would all be given the same short shrift as "culture in its own terms" (culture-as-constituted). Thus, language can only be studied as spoken, as discourse, for that is the form which language takes as social action.

A problem which others have raised bears on one of Geertz's statements in the quotation above. It is said that it is all very well to abstract culture as I have, but that this is perhaps a useless enterprise because I never show how culture is then related to behavior or social action. Thus, of what use is it to know that there is a distinction between "substance and code for conduct" since I never show how (to quote Geertz again) "cultural forms find articulation" "through the flow of . . . social action."

This criticism can be answered by recalling that the study of culture "in its own terms," as I have described it in this book, is an endeavor in which the very first step is to deal with the "flow of social action" and "actual behavior" as much as possible, or, what is the next best thing, to report what people say about what they are doing, and what they think they are doing, and why they are doing what they are doing, and above all, how they define and understand what they are doing. It is from this material—which in the case of this book is the six thousand pages of interview materials—that the symbols and meanings are abstracted. If the process of abstraction has been performed properly, and if the theory which has guided that process is not faulty, and if it is indeed symbols and meanings that have been abstracted (and this abstraction is called "culture"), then it must be both possible and legitimate to ask how those abstracted elements are related to each other and what systematic characteristics they may have. It is another, but quite different question to ask how they affect social action, or how they are articulated in social action.

If it is legitimate as well as possible to so abstract "culture" and to ask about the relationships among its elements, it is then necessary to go to the next question: How is culture articulated in social action or how does culture affect social action? or, What role does culture play in social action? This is ultimately *the* question, of course; this is what social science is for. Without that question all the rest is empty.

Is there any justification for asking just one question at a time, or asking only the question about culture, and leaving the second question untouched? I think so. First, if the process of abstraction is done correctly (and that is not always easy, as the first section of this retrospective essay suggests), it guarantees that the symbols and meanings will

be taken from the flow of social action, and therefore the abstractions
will remain implicitly true to their place in the flow of social action.
Second, if the theory which guides the abstraction is correct, then the
abstraction of culture "in its own terms" will not be one which includes
irrelevant elements. Indeed, the relevance of culture for social action is
either axiomatic or a working hypothesis. Third, to use the analogy of
language once again, if we listen to someone who speaks the sentence
"Now is the time for all good men to come to the aid of the party," we
can analyze that sentence for its grammar, syntax, etc.; we can find a
subject and a predicate, a verb and a noun, and so on. From this we
learn part of the *langue*, the language-as-constituted, but we have not
analyzed it as *parole*, language-as-spoken. We have not lost the capacity
to go back to that spoken sentence and ask what role the grammar plays
in it. Our analysis does not exhaust the sentence by any means, for we
have left out intention, among other things, in order to see the language-
as-constituted in its own terms. Nor have we got so far from the flow of
actual life as to lock cultural or grammatical and syntactic considerations
away from it.

There has been a surge of interest among linguists in discourse and
in language-as-speech, *parole*. Many linguists are interested, just as are
many anthropologists, in symbols or signs, and in meanings, and in the
relations between signs and meaning. Some have gone so far as to deny
the legitimacy of the study of *langue* and will study only *parole*. Their
results are then expressed as rules for speech and rules of reference and
consist in what appears to me to be just a bare step away from simple
empirical generalization. Instead of being able to stipulate just what
signs or symbols are embedded in the ongoing action, how those signs
are related to each other and to the different meanings, we have only a
description of the flow of action. The material cannot be analyzed in
any of the traditional senses of that word, but must be "understood" by
some hermeneutic process. All is action; pure, thick action. This I do not
accept. I am not a positivist. I am not even looking for causal connections.
But I do think that some kind of analysis is possible, that it is possible
to separate action into its constituent parts in order to see how it is constructed, and by so doing, better to understand how action proceeds.

The problem of cultural determinism and the problems of culture sui
generis are closely related to the problems I have been discussing. The
discussion has brought out my position that culture is one, but just one,
among other determinants of social action. I do not take the position
that culture is sui generis, a thing in and of itself, or that it has any
existence outside the construction of the anthropologist who builds that
structure of abstractions.

This leaves the problem of showing how the culture which I have abstracted does indeed affect, determine, or relate to action. In part, the reply is that the problems can be separated: the first problem, precisely because it has been neglected for so long, is to get at the *langue*, the competence, the culture-as-constituted. When we know as much about culture-as-constituted as we do about the structure of grammar and syntax, *langue* and competence, then we can indeed, as the linguists are doing now, go all-out for the second problem, the study of culture-in-action, pragmatics, or the study of language-as-speech. Just as the linguists use their knowledge of the phonetic system, grammar, syntax, and vocabulary in the study of pragmatics or language-as-speech, we can use our growing knowledge about the structure of signs or symbols and the structure of meaning, and the ways in which signs and meanings relate under various formally defined conditions, in the study of the ongoing pattern of life or the flow of social action, culture-as-lived. Culture will not explain everything, but it is a necessary part of the explanation.

I have been blessed with a bounty of colleagues, friends, and acquaintances, all of whom have acted as critics of one sort or another of this book. Some of them have brought repeatedly to my attention another point which bears on the problem of the relation between culture and action. The form of their criticism has been clear and direct. In this book I say as forcefully as possible that culture is not to be confused with actual patterns of action, with what people can be observed to be actually doing; nor should culture be confused with patterns *for* action (which I call norms and distinguish sharply from culture). This has left some of my critical friends and colleagues indignant, partly because I put the matter in the strongest possible terms. These statements have been interpreted—and correctly so—to mean that I am not concerned with describing actual patterns of action, what people actually do when they act out roles, what roles people actually play, or general regularities in the behavior or action of the population under study. I affirm most emphatically in Section V of the introduction (p. 18) that I am concerned with the system of symbols and meanings and not with description at any other level. The book is not about what people say (though it derives from what they say), and it is not about what people actually do or about the rates at which they do it. All this seemed quite straightforward and easily understandable when I wrote it.

The problem here is simple, really. My critics and I have different definitions of culture, different theories of social action, different objectives. Whether theirs are any more or less legitimate than mine or whether we only do different things and so do them in different ways is the question. These critics may define culture as any patterned behavior which is learned. This, to me, includes everything—the kitchen sink as well as all the plumbing.

Such a definition of culture makes it difficult to separate the meaningful from the organizational aspects of action; the motivational from the non-motivational. It lumps symbol, meaning, value, role, pattern, intention, and includes even behavior as long as it is patterned—and it is hard to find any behavior which is not patterned. It is, in a word, an imperialistic notion of culture, leaving no room for the careful discrimination of kinds of variables (sociological, psychological, etc.) or their respective places.

With different objectives, and a different definition of culture, it is not surprising that my critics object to my theory with as much vehemence as I do to theirs. I think their theory and conceptualization is faulty; they feel my theory and conceptualization are outrageously wrong. There is really a very simple solution to this difficulty, and that is to spell out the differences and to analyze carefully their implications. But this is not the place to do so. Perhaps time will tell. I have chosen to assume the significance of symbol and meaning in the total pattern of action, and to go ahead and study that. Hence, for example, I do not take rates of cross-cousin marriage as the object of my study, but only as data to be used in helping to locate the meaning of cross-cousin marriage and how it is signified.

Geertz says that meaning is "drawn from," or "cultural forms find their articulation" in "an ongoing pattern of life." These affirmations seem innocent enough. Surely meaning is no more made in heaven than marriages are; meaning must come from life somehow. But Geertz goes the step further by telling us that meaning is *not* to be found by specifying the internal relationships among the symbolic elements. This pretty well takes care of Saussure and Levi-Strauss, among others, although they might well complain about the lack of due process.

Whether meaning is drawn from action, or whether meaning is given by the use to which the signs are put is not really a problem; such statements are patently inadequate. If, to repeat yet again, social action is meaningful, symbolic, then the meaning must be in the action in the first place and cannot be "derived" from the action or "drawn from" it except in the obvious sense that if "cultural forms find their articulation" in action, and the action is symbolic and meaningful in the first place, then clearly we can recover those symbols and those meanings by analyzing the action. But the statement that meaning derives from action or from use must be wrong, in the sense that there is first the action and then the meaning emerges only after the action takes place, only after the use is established in the act. It is meaning, and the vehicles which carry it which go to form that action before it occurs, or at least, while it is occurring. We surely do not speak English as distinct from French as a derivative of the action of speech; English and French come before, and came before, any speech that anyone makes today. Its signs are drawn upon by the speaker to constitute the act of speaking, and are related to what is signified. Its meanings are there and are among the conditions which permit a speaker to choose which sign to vocalize before he speaks. He does not say "The quick red fox jumped over the lazy brown dog" when what he intended was "Please pass the salt," for he knows that the word "salt" is nowhere easily related to quick red fox or lazy brown dog. And what is just as important is the fact that if he really wants the salt, he won't get it, no matter how often he repeats "The quick red fox jumped over the lazy brown dog." The actor has intentions; they are customary, generally shared structures of signs and what they signify so that he can not only indicate his intentions, but have some reasonable assurance that he will not be whistling in the dark. It is conceivable that he might eventually succeed through some other channel of communication—perhaps he points to the salt cellar; perhaps he reaches out and picks it up seven times, each time uttering the sentence "The quick red fox jumped over the lazy brown dog" so that after a while people get the idea that this peculiar, idiosyncratic speaker making those noises, should be passed the salt. Then and only then can it be said with any legitimacy that "use" is what the meaning is drawn from. But even then, it is not simply use, but the establishment of a consensus among the community of speakers and hearers that in this situation, for this speaker, "The quick red fox jumped over the lazy brown dog" should be used to mean "Please pass the salt."

There is a system of signs and meanings which everyone has to learn as a child and must continue to learn even as an adult, and this is not simply an edict of any individual actor. It is precisely this system of signs and meanings that is "out there" that I call culture—culture-as-constituted. But "out there" is only a way of saying that if an observer watches and listens to what goes on he will be able to abstract from that ongoing flow of life certain regularities which are generally agreed relations between sign and meaning in this community. These relations are not "out there" as objects, as reified entities which can be felt, smelt, and tasted. They are constructions of abstractions built by an observer and it is in this sense alone that they are "out there." It is those parts of ongoing action which can be shown to be signs and meanings which are conventionally associated. Further, any newcomer to the community, adult or child, must learn these conventional associations before he can do more than behave, that is, before his behavior can be regarded as social action.

It is precisely those dimensions or signs and their meanings which can be abstracted as previously constituted which I treat as culture. Even highly context specific or context dependent signs derive a part of their meaning from the constituted, or previously constituted culture. To turn the whole matter around, as can be seen from the analysis in this book, I use not only relatively context free material, but also highly context sensitive material from which to abstract the culture-as-constituted material with which I am concerned.

Occasionally I am told, "The main trouble with your book and your theory is that you don't understand that *all* meaning is context sensitive. You assume that meaning is absolute and does not depend on context, and that is just wrong." It is clear that such a speaker misunderstands both the object and the method of my enterprise. I know just as well as he does that all meaning is more or less context dependent. And knowing that, I am able to use both the more, as well as the less context dependent material I encounter in field work to abstract those aspects of even the most context sensitive rules for action, and from this, to abstract the culture-as-constituted and go on to construct the abstract system which I call "culture."

This point is significant because from the very first my objection to not only componential analysis, but to all of those forms of the treatment of "kinship" and "kinship terms" which anthropologists have pursued with unremitting vigor, is precisely that they fail to take large masses of data into account. They confine themselves to the so-called "referential" terminology, ignoring vocative forms; they ignore different usages; they ignore alternate forms; they ignore what they call "metaphorical extension." My criticism is precisely that it is not just in the narrow referential usages alone that the meaning of "kinship" lies, but that there are many other constituted elements, valued elements which need to be taken into account. And in this book, for example, my discussion of the different forms of "father" (pop, dad, etc.) and the problem of the aunt and uncle by marriage are precisely to the point. Here are exquisitely context dependent usages which cannot be ignored if one is trying, as I have, to construct a model of culture-as-constituted.

I have already noted that my definition of culture as a system of symbols and meanings differs from other definitions, especially those which treat culture in the most general terms as patterns of learned behavior— all patterned behavior, or all learned or socially transmitted behavior.

But there is another significant difference between the definition of culture which I use and many others. This is my distinction between culture as a system of symbols and meanings, and *norms* as patterns of and for behavior. Or, to characterize norms in a different way, as the rules for action. In the introduction to *American Kinship* I deal with this distinction in less detail than I should have; it is explained more fully in "Notes Toward a Theory of Culture."

Norms are, of course, actor-oriented and action-oriented; they specify the roles which should be played under designated circumstances by actors occupying designated statuses or categories. The system of symbols and meanings of a culture can be abstracted from these norms, because in the norms there is an implicit classification of categories, sets of presuppositions about the state of affairs, the conditions of life, cosmology, and so on which provide the materials from which the system of symbols and meanings can be drawn. Thus norms are not in themselves *simply* patterns of and for action; they consist of cultural elements as well. Thus there is a cultural aspect to norms as well as an action aspect. But where a cosmology, for example, is oriented to the state of the world or the universe, a normative system is oriented to patterns for action by socially defined persons.

Since I have subscribed to the Parsonian position that the social system is quite distinct from the cultural system, it follows that I must class norms, insofar as they are treated as patterns for action, as part of the social system and separate those aspects from the cultural system.

The traditional view has been to view action as an indivisible unit which is the major constituent of culture. Hence those who take this position find my treatment of American "kinship" deficient in just what they are eager to know—in the words of that famous old limerick, who does what with which and to whom under what conditions.

My treatment of culture in this book, as elsewhere, has been based consistently on the view of culture as a total system. The standard of reference for any relationship of signifier and signified has been culture-as-constituted. But this treatment is quite different from one which takes the actor as the point of reference and asks, for example, "How should a father behave?" or "What is the role of the mother in such and such a situation?" Here the standard of reference is not directly that of the cultural system-as-constituted, but is instead that of the actor in action. The more extreme variant of this position is taken by those who use some form of decision-making theory and ask, for example, "What do I need to know in order to act like a native (father, mother, etc.)?"

And here again the fundamental distinction between culture-as-lived and culture-as-constituted becomes crucial. Various difficulties arise with an actor-oriented perspective. The first and most obvious is that it is not system-oriented, as is the culture-as-constituted view. The second is that it obscures what I hold to be vital: the important distinction between social organization or social system and culture. To fail to maintain this distinction leads to the reduction of culture to social organization (or social structure) or to the opposite difficulty, the imperialist view of culture, namely, that culture includes and comprehends the social system and social organization. Here the social system is but a part of culture, and this means that culture includes virtually everything, so that the leverage in analysis of the distinction between relevant variables is lost.

But the most profound difficulty with the failure to distinguish the system-oriented from the actor-oriented view is the kind of functional analyses which have resulted from the confusion of the two. What I have called either "the band-aid theory" or the "exuvium theory" of ritual and magic is a case in point. Treating magic as a way of reducing anxiety contingent on the inability to control the unknown rests precisely on the conflation of the system- and the actor-oriented modes of analysis. These theories depend upon a state of affairs generated in the culture or the social structure (however they are defined) which create the conditions motivating actors to create and re-create modes of adaptation to those circumstances. Not only does this shift the burden of causality to the social organization and make of magic and ritual mere poultices on, or mere exuvia of, the social structure or culture, but it rests on the premise that ritual and magic are exempted from the culture-as-constituted, and must be regarded only as culture-as-acted, or more precisely, culture as re-action.

It has been said that my use of a distinctive feature type of analysis was a mistake. Given the importance of signs as indexical, of pragmatics, or culture-as-lived or culture-in-action, a distinctive feature analysis was just the wrong way to go about things.

If I were doing pragmatics or culture-as-lived, then indeed a distinctive feature analysis might be the wrong way to go about it. But I am doing, as I have said before, a different kind of analysis. I am doing a kind of analysis that is close to the kind that the linguist does when he tries to establish a phonemic system, to locate the phonemes and their relation to each other. Phonemes, and a phonemic system, are precisely sounds-as-meaningfully-constituted rather than a sounds-as-spoken system. A distinctive feature analysis is aimed at bringing out the valorized dimensions in terms of the differences among them. That these are, or can be, set in terms of oppositions of a plus and minus sort, or a present/absent sort with respect to certain specified dimensions—voicing, glottalization, and so forth—is closer to the kind of cultural analysis at which

I aim than the elaborate specification of the different rules for making the various sounds under various conditions of speech and in different contexts of actual speaking. Much more could be said about distinctive feature analysis, for it is used by Scheffler and Lounsbury and has been used by other practicing "componential analysts" with whom I have serious intellectual differences. In a full discussion I should specify precisely when I mean by a distinctive feature analysis and where I differ from the ways in which the componential analysts have used it, but such a discussion would lead us too far afield. The book itself shows just how I use it.

Another criticism which this book has met with is that the book may perhaps locate symbols and meanings, but that different kinds of relations between signifier and signified, between symbol and meaning, and between different kinds of symbols are not fully allowed for and certainly not fully explored. It is conceded that the idea of an "epitomizing" symbol tried to do this in part, but that it is not enough: the distinction between iconic and indexical signs is not used. The relationship between different signs as being derived from other signs is not touched. The idea of metaphor and metonym is not mentioned, while in other papers it is vehemently denied.

I accept this criticism as just. It is true. I have been of many minds about the problems of metaphor and metonym; about primary meaning; about extension of meaning. I find the definition of polysemy as a set of meanings in which there is one from which all others in the set derive unsatisfactory, and so I use a simple definition of polysemy as a multiplicity of meanings without stating the relationship among them.

The fundamental distinction between culture-as-constituted and culture-in-action or culture-as-lived is useful in helping to understand my position in another matter. I hold that a significant part of the meaning of the elements of a culture depends on their relation to each other in a system of oppositions or contrasts. Here my position is close to Levi-Strauss and before him, Saussure. To them, meaning, in the special sense in which they and I use the term, is precisely the idea or the concept of the sign *in its relation to other signs within the same system*. It is not the reference of the sign to something in the world.

It is also important to note that this system has the qualities of markedness and hierarchy. Just how these in turn relate to my contention that the total system can be shown to be organized around a small set of epitomizing symbols is a problem which I am not prepared to deal with here, for it requires extended and detailed discussion. Suffice it to say that I would stand by my contention that if the proposition can be accepted that culture-as-constituted can be seen as a *system* or a *struc-*

ture, and that the system or structure is defined by the relations among
its elements, then one of those kinds of relations can be expected to be
such that certain elements in certain relations have valorization which
puts them in a privileged position. This is not more than merely to assert
once again that every culture-as-constituted can, I believe, be shown to
be organized around such a small core of epitomizing symbols.

REFERENCES

Barnett, S., and Silverman, M.G. 1979. "Separations in Capitalist Societies:
    Persons, Things, Units, and Relations." In *Ideology and Everyday Life*.
    Ann Arbor: University of Michigan Press.
Craig, D. "Immortality through Kinship: The Vertical Transmission of
    Substance and Symbolic Estate." *American Anthropologist* 81 (1979):
    94.
Dolgin, J.; Kemnitzer, D.; and Schneider, D. M. *Symbolic Anthropology*.
    New York: Columbia University Press, 1977.
Geertz, C. *The Interpretation of Cultures*. New York: Basic Books, 1973.
Sahlins, M. "Individual Experience and Cultural Order." Manuscript,
    1979.
Schneider, D. M. 1955. "Kinship Terminology and the American Kinship
    System." *American Anthropologist* 57:1194–1208.
———. 1961. "Sibling Solidarity: A Property of American Kinship." *Amer-
    ican Anthropologist* 63:489–507 (Cummings and Schneider).
———. 1965. "American Kin Terms and Terms for Kinsmen: A Critique
    of Goodenough's Componential Analysis of Yankee Terminology." In
    "Formal Semantic Analysis," edited by E. A. Hammel, pp. 288–308.
    American Anthropologist 67, part 2.
———. 1969. "Kinship, Nationality and Religion in American Culture:
    Toward a Definition of Kinship." In *Forms of Symbolic Action,* edited
    by V. Turner, pp. 116–25. *Proceedings of the 1969 Annual Spring Meet-
    ing of the American Ethnological Society.*
———. 1970. "American Kin Categories." In *Echanges et Communications:
    Mélanges offerts à Claude Lévi-Strauss,* edited by P. Maranda and J.
    Pouillon, pp. 370–81. The Hague: Mouton.
———. 1972. "What is Kinship all About?" In *Kinship Studies in the
    Morgan Centennial Year,* edited by P. Reining, pp. 32–63. Washington,
    D.C.: Washington Anthropological Society.
———. 1973. *Class Differences in American Kinship*. Ann Arbor: Univer-
    sity of Michigan Press. Reprinted 1978 (Schneider and Smith).
———. 1975. "Kinship Vis-a-vis Myth." *American Anthropologist* 76:799–
    817 (Boon and Schneider).

———. 1975. *The American Kin Universe: A Genealogical Study*. Chicago: University of Chicago Publications in Anthropology (Schneider and Cottrell).

———. 1976. "Notes Toward a Theory of Culture." In *Meaning in Anthropology*, edited by K. Basso and H. Selby. Albuquerque: University of New Mexico Press.

———. 1979. "Kinship, Community and Locality in American Culture." In *Kin and Communities*, edited by A. J. Lichtman and J. R. Challinor, pp. 155–74. Washington, D.C.: Smithsonian Press.

———. Forthcoming. *A Critique of the Study of Kinship*. Ann Arbor: University of Michigan Press.

Yanagisako, S. J. "Variations in American Kinship: Implications for Cultural Analysis." *American Ethnologist* 5 (1978):15–29